T0356297

Praise for *Stewards Not Owners*

God's Word has a lot to say about money, but it can be difficult knowing how to apply those truths to our twenty-first-century materialistic culture. Thankfully, Bill and Dana Wichterman have laid out a clear, accessible framework for believers who want to manage their personal resources in a way that honors God and furthers His kingdom. I know many families will learn to steward their finances joyfully and faithfully after reading *Stewards Not Owners*.

> —Jim Daly, president of Focus on the Family

The principles that Dana and Bill share in this important book are a guide to making sure that how you manage your money will contribute to your journey in faith, rather than be an impediment to it. Our family has lived by these principles and can attest to their soundness.

> —Andrew Abela, PhD, dean of The Busch School of
> Business, The Catholic University of America

I wholeheartedly encourage you to read and apply the biblical principles, practical insights, and life experiences you are about to explore in the pages ahead.

> —Chuck Bentley, CEO of Crown Financial Ministries and
> founder of Christian Economic Forum

What a gift! This book on money is inspiring, insightful and wise. The authors share their years of prayer, reading, and talking with others as they call us on the exciting adventure of generous living as fully devoted disciples of Christ. Come and join the adventure!

> —Baroness Stroud, CEO of ARC, member of the House of
> Lords and cofounder of Forum, and Rev. David Stroud,
> founding pastor of Christ Church London, cofounder of
> Forum and cofounder of the Everything Network

Being a Christian is not the secret to happiness on earth. But as Dana and Bill Wichterman show, *giving* like a Christian just might be. Read *Stewards Not Owners* and start your journey to a better life.

> —Arthur C. Brooks, Harvard professor and #1 *New York
> Times* bestselling author

Dana and Bill Wichterman combine a powerful personal testimony of joyful stewardship with an immensely practical guide for others who also long to hear the words "well done." Their invitation to leverage all our resources—including our investment portfolios—to multiply God's kingdom is an important and timely challenge. I hope Dana and Bill's story leads many others to find the joy and peace they've found in freely stewarding God's resources.

—J. D. Greear, PhD, pastor of The Summit Church

The deepest, truest learning is always over the shoulder, and through the heart. In this wisely written and wonderfully imagined book, Dana and Bill Wichterman invite us to their pilgrimage into the meaning of life and labor, the marketplace and money. From beginning to end we are graced with their serious joy as they discover a more profoundly coherent life, twining their most important beliefs about all that matters most with the responsibility of their growing resources. *Stewards Not Owners* is both the story of the challenge of their own lifelong stewardship as well as the stories of their community of friends whose hearts have taken them all over the world, in their own very different ways each longing to love what God loves in and through a vision of generous giving.

—Steven Garber, author of *The Seamless Life: A Tapestry of Love and Learning, Worship and Work,* and senior fellow for Vocation and the Common Good, M. J. Murdock Charitable Trust

We live life, John Calvin said, *coram deo* . . . or, before the face of God. Further, it is His world, not ours. So, to be human is to *steward what is not our own.* That's what this book is about: stewarding life as if everything belongs to God, because it does. But this book, through stories and straightforward simplicity, is also an *invitation* to think of stewardship in terms of generosity. It's a compelling vision, one Dana and Bill have long embraced and now share.

—John Stonestreet, president of the Colson Center and coauthor of *A Practical Guide to Culture*

Most of the books written about financial stewardship seem to be authored by those who have a vested interest in our giving more. They tend to be preaching and proscriptive, filled with too-good-to-be-real promises—and sometimes threats. Not so with Dana and

Bill Wichterman's book. This is a book of stories that are not only true, but also personal. Just as Jesus used parables to illustrate a point, Dana and Bill have compiled stories to illustrate principles. Parables did not just indict, they also encouraged. The same holds true for *Stewards Not Owners*. You will, as I did, find yourself saying, "Yes, that is what I want in my own life."

—Fred Smith, founder of The Gathering

Stewards Not Owners is one of the most unique and remarkable books on Christian finances that I've come across. Told through captivating, real-life stories, Dana and Bill Wichterman bring the principles of stewardship to life in a way that is both practical, inspiring, and uplifting. Their approach goes beyond the usual financial advice, touching on important but often overlooked topics like investing for impact, making this a truly worthwhile guide for anyone genuinely seeking to align their money with their faith. I highly recommend this book for those ready to live out Christian stewardship with purpose and intentionality.

—Pastor John K. Jenkins, Sr., First Baptist Church of Glenarden

Stewards Not Owners is a thoughtful, practical, and faithful book about financial stewardship. But it's not just a series of arguments; it is also a collection of powerful stories and profiles. Dana and Bill Wichterman are teaching Christians what it means to align finances with faith. This book doesn't rely on scolding people into generosity; it relies instead on inspiring them, especially by profiling faithful stewards. Their stories show what generosity looks like in flesh-and-blood.

—Peter Wehner, contributing opinion writer for *The New York Times*

For anyone seeking to creatively and faithfully steward their resources, *Stewards Not Owners* is a godsend. Dana and Bill Wichterman—themselves inspiring examples of bold, generative stewardship—offer profound insights on aligning your money with your faith through the real-life stories of faithful stewards. Wise, accessible, and rich in practical guidance, this work is also an inspiring call to joy and flourishing through generous living.

—Cherie Harder, president of The Trinity Forum

Sociologist Max Weber coined the phrase "'Protestant work ethic'" to describe a sense of vocation that drives Christians to work hard, but to avoid conspicuous consumption—leading to the accumulation of wealth that can be given to creative or charitable projects. In *Stewards Not Owners*, Dana and Bill Wichterman spell out what that work ethic looks like in everyday life, offering tips and truths on how to donate and invest money in a responsible manner. The book is a delightful read, blending personal stories with biblical principles and solid financial insights. It will inspire you to be more intentional about using your own resources to better serve God and advance His purposes in the world.

> —Nancy Pearcey, professor and scholar in residence at Houston Christian University, author of *Total Truth, Finding Truth,* and *Love Thy Body*

Stewards Not Owners is compelling reading, full of fascinating stories and challenging to any believer who wants to be faithful to their Lord. This book deserves to be read by any follower of Jesus. The Wichtermans, along with the twenty-four kingdom leaders they interview, show brilliant and creative solutions to giving that multiply resources in ways that help, not hurt, the poor. You will want to read this book all the way through and share it with friends.

> —Rev. Dr. Art Lindsley, author of *C. S. Lewis's Case for Christ*

In *Stewards Not Owners*, Dana and Bill Wichterman present an inspiring approach to finances you wish your parents had told you from the start. This book goes beyond the occasional sermon on generosity, overturns the heavy-handed moralism that shames wealth, and undermines the name-it-claim-it approach to finances—instead it calls you to something radically different than what everyone else is doing: a joyful, kingdom approach to money.

> —Nancy French, author of *Ghosted: An American Story*

Dana and Bill Wichterman have given us a wonderfully crafted, witty, down-to-earth, practical handbook chronicling the stories of people who have surrendered their finances to God. Read *Stewards Not Owners*, put it into practice, and you, too, can experience joy through the biblical stewardship of God's gifts.

> —Joel Woodruff, president of the C. S. Lewis Institute

Dana and Bill Wichterman have captured powerful stories of God's people stewarding their resources to God's glory. They make a compelling case that surrendering all that we have and are to God brings us closer to Christ. *Stewards Not Owners* will capture your heart and mind as it invites you into a joyful journey of generosity.

—Howard Dayton, founder of Crown Financial Ministries and Compass–Finances God's Way

While reading *Stewards Not Owners*, I was challenged, encouraged, and inspired by the varied and compelling examples of twenty-four thoughtful people giving their lives away for the sake of others. In writing this book, Dana and Bill have provided a road map to a life of meaning, purpose, and joy in handling God's resources open-handedly and strategically.

—Todd Harper, cofounder of Generous Giving

Money is a complex topic for Christians, a blessing that can very easily be a curse. In *Stewards Not Owners*, Dana and Bill Wichterman share their deep, hard-won, and often personal reflections on the habits, mindsets, and values that can make wealth a tool for good in the life of any believer.

—John Coleman, Co-CEO of Sovereign's Capital

This book will delight, inspire, convict, and motivate. In a world in which most of us have to go looking for heroes, Dana and Bill Wichterman went out and found them—twenty-four examples of amazing, self-giving, beautiful souls who have embarked on a daring adventure to acknowledge God's ownership of everything: their resources, their talents, and their very lives. Its message is made all the more powerful in knowing that its authors exemplify the book's message through their own lives of remarkable dedication to God.

—Don Eberly, former White House aide, author, and social entrepreneur

To tell our stories more truly requires that we take money seriously, and hence, the God who invented it. For indeed, what we do with money reflects the degree to which we are being formed into the image of the Jesus of generosity. With *Stewards Not Owners*, Dana and Bill Wichterman have provided a rich collection of stories of those people whose lives have been transformed by God on the way to their becoming wellsprings of wisdom and that very generosity.

Read this book and walk through the door through which God is inviting you to join Him in His mission to joyfully transform your life into a generous gift to others.

—Curt Thompson, MD, psychiatrist and author of *The Soul of Desire* and *The Deepest Place*

Some books inspire but leave you hanging on what to do next. Others are so practical they are akin to a college textbook. Not so with *Stewards Not Owners*. Dana and Bill beautifully weave together well-told, real-life stories that will cause you to lean in, with very practical pointers that will equip you to step in.

—Andrew Scott, founder of SCATTER

Through twenty-four engaging stories, the Wichtermans show the joy that comes from aligning our view of money through the lens of faith. God desires to be intimately involved in our lives and that includes our stewardship of finances, and how that impacts a believer in a holistic way from saving, spending, investments, work, and retirement.

—Jess Correll, founder of First Southern National Bank and Angela Correll, author of *Restored in Tuscany*

Stewards Not Owners is full of wisdom and joy from a couple who knows how to make giving fun.

—Steve Taylor, recording artist and filmmaker

This is a couple's engaging thirty-five-year journey of stewardship. Such insight can only come from real life experiences. Humility is displayed as you journey with Dana and Bill through their many stories and stimulating examples. It is sure to impact and influence you! As a field guide of stewardship, it will help prepare you to stand before the Lord to receive a commendation!

—Raymond H. Harris, architect, venture capitalist in God's kingdom, executive movie producer, and author of *Business by Design* and *Enduring Wealth*

Stewards Not Owners is divine guidance for believers who have a conviction for seeing the standards and promises of God for finances manifested in their lives. The life stories of Dana and Bill uniquely qualify them as authors. The testimonies shared of others are truly inspiring. Those who are committed to seeing God's standards and promises for finances manifest in their lives will gain practical, near-term, and strategic insights into examining the use of their money and aligning their finances with their faith. The principles of stewardship presented are deeper than I have ever considered, such as examining how your money is being used by others you trust to invest it, making sure it is being used in ways that honor the Lord and building His kingdom. I wish it had been written thirty years ago!

—Dr. Kelvin J. Cochran, former US fire administrator and author of *Facing the Fire*

Money and wealth are beautiful, good gifts of God, and simultaneously fallen lures to idolatry. Dana and Bill Wichterman wisely hold this tension by exploring biblical teaching, sharing their own personal journeys, and telling the stewardship stories of others. This is an important book, demonstrating that there is joy in being faithful stewards of the resources God places in our hands.

—Dennis P. Hollinger, PhD, president emeritus and senior distinguished professor of Christian Ethics at Gordon-Conwell Theological Seminary

Dana and Bill provide a thoughtful, practical, biblical approach to thinking about financial stewardship. They aptly make the point that neither being driven by the accumulation of wealth nor eschewing consideration of financial stewardship is an appropriate route for Christians to take. Instead, they provide principles and anecdotes to inform and inspire stewardship and generosity as part of living out our Christian faith.

—Dr. Wayne Lewis, president of Houghton University

As the president of a Christian university, I have the privilege of watching faculty members integrate their disciplines with their faith. It's our priority to teach students how every part of their worlds and every part of their lives can be transformed by God's beauty, truth, and goodness. Faith integration done well can be life changing. Dana and my friend Bill apply the same type of integrative mindset to financial stewardship, unveiling the beauty of—and the practical steps we can take toward—inviting God fully into our financial dealings, and, in turn, our lives. This is not just financial advice with a Christian gloss, it is a deeply Christian book.

—Barry H. Corey, PhD, president of Biola University and author of *Love Kindness* and *Make the Most of It*

Dana and Bill Wichterman have crafted a timely and insightful guide to understanding the true essence of stewardship. In *Stewards Not Owners*, they take us beyond the clichés by drawing from Scripture and faithful believers' experiences to provide clarity on financial discernment. Whether you are new to the journey of stewardship or seeking a revolutionary new paradigm, this book will inspire and challenge you to live with open hands and a heart for the Gospel.

—D. Michael Lindsay, president of Taylor University

This book was a pleasure to read, not just because it is well written, but more importantly, because it is grounded in what Scripture teaches about whole life stewardship. And it illustrates those truths with inspiring examples and practical guidance that can help readers enter into the freedom and joy that comes from using their gifts, abilities, and resources for God's glory. C. S. Lewis, who was a faithful steward and generous giver himself, would have loved it!

—Thomas Tarrants, president emeritus of the
　　C. S. Lewis Institute

I'm very upset with the Wichtermans. Why couldn't they have written this book years ago? They might have dissuaded me from my passionate determination to become the greatest financial dunderhead the world has ever known. The Wichtermans encourage us to be generous, wise, and, above all, joyful in doing so. To me this is exciting and liberating. You'll get no "name and claim it" prosperity doctrine nonsense here. It's never too late for us to wise up and, with God's help, do better.

—Terry Scott Taylor, singer, songwriter, and producer

Ecclesiastes 4:9 says: "Two are better than one, because they have a good reward for their labor." Dana and Bill have been rewarded by their faithful stewardship, living wisely and generously. Their reward? Knowing that because they have heeded the parable of the talents, the Lord will say to them, "Well done, good and faithful servants." Their book is an encouragement to us to labor for the same.

—Mark Rodgers, founder of Wedgwood Circle and former
　　senior congressional staff member

STEWARDS
NOT
OWNERS

The Joy of
Aligning Your Money
with Your Faith

STEWARDS
NOT
OWNERS

The Joy of
Aligning Your Money
with Your Faith

Dana and Bill Wichterman

Forefront
BOOKS

No patent liability is assumed with respect to the use of the information contained herein. Although every precaution has been taken in the preparation of this book, the publisher and author assume no responsibility for errors or omissions. Neither is any liability assumed for damages resulting from the use of the information contained herein.

This book is intended for informational purposes only. It is not intended to be used as the sole basis for financial or investing decisions, nor should it be construed as advice designed to meet the particular needs of an individual's situation.

All proceeds from book sales will go to Faith Driven Investor, Generous Giving, and Impact Foundation.

Published by Forefront Books, Nashville, Tennessee.
Distributed by Simon & Schuster.

Unless otherwise noted, Scripture quotations are from the Holy Bible, New International Version®, NIV®, Copyright © 1973, 1978, 1984, 2011 by Biblica, Inc.™ Used by permission of Zondervan. All rights reserved worldwide.

Scripture quotations marked ESV are from the ESV® Bible (The Holy Bible, English Standard Version®). Copyright © 2001 by Crossway, a publishing ministry of Good News Publishers. All rights reserved.

Scripture quotations marked KJV are from the King James Version. Public domain.

Library of Congress Control Number: 2024926458

Print ISBN: 978-1-63763-375-5
E-book ISBN: 978-1-63763-376-2

Cover Design by Bruce Gore, Gore Studio, Inc.
Interior Design by PerfecType, Nashville, TN

Printed in the United States of America

DEDICATION

Dedicated to Henry and Kimberley Kaestner, April and Craig Chapman, and Dennis and Eileen Bakke, each of whom has modeled for us a life surrendered to Jesus.

CONTENTS

FOREWORD

What words do you want to hear when you die and stand before the Lord?

Need a second to think about it?

For the past twenty-four years, during the hundreds and hundreds of public talks I have given before live audiences of Christians around the world, I have taken an informal survey using those two questions.

My guess is that just like those in the audiences that I have surveyed, you may have your reply on the tip of your tongue. You likely did not hesitate to know what you would say aloud if I asked you the same question. The universal answer I always get is, "Well done, good and faithful servant."

My follow-up question is, "Where does it say that in the Bible?"

That is when the room gets quiet.

The audience usually gets even quieter when I ask, "What does a Christian need to do to hear those words?" or "What is the parable of the talents in Matthew 25 actually about?" or "Since it is a conditional promise related to money and possessions, what conditions do I need to meet?"

Certainly, I would have found myself with a blank stare if asked those same follow-on questions in 1999, even though, as a middle-aged Christian husband, father, and businessman, I had attended church and read my Bible since I was seven years old. As much as I would have sincerely desired to hear those wonderful words of affirmation from the Lord Jesus Christ, I had not been trained to be an intentional steward of resources.

True biblical stewardship is not ordering your finances in such a way that you can freely spend money however you want; rather, it is ordering your finances in such a way that God can freely spend you however He wants. Only by dying to the power that money wields over our lives can we become fully alive and useful to the Lord.

To understand what it means to be a steward is to understand God's operating system. It is the way He designed us to function at our very best. Certainly, it is a novice idea that stewardship is simply paying off debt, cutting up credit cards, or living on a budget. It is also far more than surrendering our claim to ownership of our stuff (money and possessions); even the unfaithful servant with just one talent recognized that God owned his talent. The deeper understanding is to acknowledge that nothing we have belongs to us—not even ourselves! God's steward acknowledges that we were bought and paid for with the precious blood of Christ and are living sacrifices to be used for His purposes, whether we have great or small resources and talents.

Money has a spiritual power as a false god or an idol. It pretends to give us an identity, security, purpose, meaning, and power. Jesus said we cannot serve Him and money. The competition for control of our lives is so great that He said we would love one and hate the other. Years ago, I came to realize which one I truly loved—money. When I made the discovery through a Crown Bible study offered in my local church, I confessed my idolatry to the Lord and repented of my love of money. Tears flowed from my eyes as the freedom and joy of serving only one Master flooded my heart. My life changed forever.

Regardless of your starting point or lifetime of experience managing money as God's steward, there is rich content ahead for beginners and veterans alike. Not only are Bill and Dana thorough and transparent about their personal journey, but you will also meet a variety of people who are remarkable stewards! Their resolve to live contrary to the world's standards for financial success will inspire and instruct you, just as they have the Wichtermans and me.

The practice of faithfully managing all the resources, gifts, and talents that God generously provides to us will not only ensure you will hear "Well done, good and faithful servant." He will also say, "You have been faithful over a little; I will set you over much. Enter into the joy of your master" (Matthew 25:23 ESV). This is a reward of eternal worth beyond our ability to imagine.

That is why I wholeheartedly encourage you to read and apply the biblical principles, practical insights, and life experiences you are about to explore in the pages ahead.

Chuck Bentley
September 2024
Knoxville, TN
CEO, Crown Financial Ministries
Founder, Christian Economic Forum
Author of *Freedom from Poverty and Riches: The Remarkable Story of Crown's Mission to Spread Financial Freedom Across the World*

INTRODUCTION

Keep your lives free from the love of money and
be content with what you have, because God has
said, "Never will I leave you; never will I forsake
you."

—Hebrews 13:5

Like most married couples, we started at the bottom.
Dana was between jobs with no income. Bill was working long hours in the US Congress for $20,000 a year. We had no car, no savings, $13,000 in school debt (which felt like a lot more thirty-five years ago), and very ugly and very old furniture. Our one-bedroom apartment was nice enough—if you didn't mind cockroaches. When we sat down to produce our first budget in the weeks after we got married, we were totally depressed. The outlook was bleak.

Thankfully, those days didn't last long. Once Dana got a full-time job working for the US Agency for International Development, we scraped together the down payment for an old Ford Tempo—that our relatives mocked—and began our climb up to a net worth of zero, which we hit three years later, just as Bill finished graduate school. (We kept that old Ford for a long time, even after we had to start using tacks to keep the ceiling liner from hanging down on our heads. Once the tacks began falling on our first child in her car seat, we finally gave it up.)

We smile looking back at those character-building days, and we also remember something else: the joy of connecting our faith in Christ to our financial stewardship. We began to understand that what we did with our money mattered to God. We still had a lot to learn, but we began with the belief that God wanted to be Lord of all we had, even though it would take many years to develop a more comprehensive view of the breadth of God's concern not just for our giving, spending, and saving but also for our investing.

It's easy to think God cares only about evangelism, missions, Bible study, and prayer, and that money just isn't His thing. Some people separate Jesus as *Savior* (something you need to confess if you want to make it into heaven) and Jesus as *Lord* (something only for "upper-level Christians," like it's an elective course you can choose not to take). So, when it comes to money, many Christians believe tithing ten percent is plenty—more than enough, in fact. Living is expensive and inflation is high. Surely, God must understand that putting kids through college these days is rough, and giving away too much money just isn't reasonable. Plus, how else can we be prepared for retirement? These days, we tell ourselves, dropping an occasional twenty in the offering plate and filling green-and-red shoe boxes with Dollar Store gifts to send overseas at Christmas is fine. It's *enough*.

If this is what you're thinking, this book might make you feel uncomfortable—but we assure you, we're pointing you to a life-giving journey. As one friend who read an early draft told us, "This book isn't just about money; it's about surrendering everything to God." Yes! And surrender entails everything, including all your money—your savings, spending, investing, and giving.

We hope you'll surrender all you are and all you have to Him. This means something quite different than giving away all your money in a once-and-done fashion—something that would be irresponsible for most people. Instead, it means learning how to wisely use all your money to please God.

Before you close the book because you think it's written by a couple of unrealistic Jesus freaks who don't live in the real world, here's what we're *not* saying:

- We're not saying you should give all your money to the church.
- We're not saying you should live an ascetic lifestyle without having any fun.
- We're not saying you should give away absolutely everything you own and then pray for God to give you back what you need to survive.

We don't live that way, and we doubt God is calling you to that path either.

This book *is* an invitation to use your money to lead an exciting and joyful life. Money is an important expression of how we follow Jesus. It's one form of power that God gives us to shape the world. With money, we can set free children who have been shackled in human trafficking and slaves who are forced to roll cigarettes twelve hours a day in India. With money, we can take vacations, eat out, build swimming pools and businesses, and pay kids' college tuition. With money, we can give to our church, pay for friends' lunches, and fund missionaries. Money matters.

Here's another thing we're *not* saying in the book: that nonprofit charities are bad. Between us, we serve on six nonprofit boards because we believe in their important work. Nonprofits have a critical role to play in human flourishing. But you'll also read that we think business as a means of advancing God's kingdom has been underappreciated. As a corrective, we will point out the limitations of nonprofits and comparative advantages of business in addressing human needs, but we don't want you to think we don't love the work so many nonprofits do. Same with government: it has a God-appointed role to play. As a couple, we worked in government for almost forty years. Every sphere—nonprofit, for-profit, and government—has been marred by sin, and we'll be arguing for a more redemptive approach to advancing God's purposes in the world.

One more note: this book is for all Christ-followers—rich, poor, and everyone in between. There may be some parts that apply less to you in your current situation, but most people will find that the principles in the book hold true for anyone seeking to align their money with their faith.

Our Story

When we read books, we like to know something about the author so we can get a sense of who we're listening to. So, here's a little more about us and our story.

Dana grew up in Denver, Colorado, the oldest child in a well-to-do, loving Christian family that acted like they were poor. Her mother set the pace for penurious living, which even included washing and reusing sandwich bags! The family lived in a nice home in a wealthy suburb, but they spent money sparingly. When they *did* go out to eat occasionally, all the kids understood they should not order the most expensive meal or a dessert, and everyone drank tap water.

Her dad, a CPA at a large accounting firm, was a risk-taker when it came to investments. He invested on margin—meaning he borrowed money to make large investments. When the bottom dropped out of the Denver economy in the early 1980s and the country descended into a recession, Dana's family was financially underwater. That experience has deeply shaped Dana's aversion to debt and her fundamentally conservative approach to money. Consequently, we live with very conservative assumptions about our economic future, and we have multiple financial safety nets below what may look like a high-wire act to a casual observer of our investing.

Dana grew up with a deep care for the poor. We both read Ron Sider's classic book *Rich Christians in an Age of Hunger*[1] around age twenty before we met each other. Dana's visit to India as a college student on a round-the-world voyage called Semester at Sea was pivotal in giving her a passion for empowering the poor. She changed her major at Denver University to international affairs and headed toward a career in international poverty alleviation, later earning a master's degree in international development from Columbia University. She spent her career at the US Agency for International Development, which administers the US foreign aid program, before staying home to raise three spirited kids. After the kids were grown, she returned to the workforce and took a job for Impact Foundation, where she currently works (more on that later).

Dana developed a life-changing condition called fibromyalgia just three months after our marriage. She's lived in constant and often debilitating pain for thirty-five years. She hates to talk about her condition, and we wrestled with whether to include this fact in the book. But it's had such an enormous impact on our view of God, suffering, and heaven, and it's formed in us a deep aversion to an unbiblical "happy-clappy" Christianity that glosses over the world's suffering and distorts God into a divine bellhop who fixes every problem for those who have faith. Dana's suffering, in which Bill partially shares through the corresponding responsibilities he's had to bear (often acting like a single parent to compensate for what Dana couldn't do), has shaped our lives and our approach to life, including finances.

Bill grew up in a middle-class Christian home in Lancaster, Pennsylvania (no, he's not Amish, though they were his neighbors), the son of two loving parents who openly discussed money and faithfully tithed each week. His family didn't go into debt, but they also weren't exactly *savers*.

After giving his life to the Lord at sixteen, Bill planned to be a pastor or a missionary, and he spent one year in short-term missions after graduating from Houghton University. Instead, the Lord led him to a political career, and for twenty years he served in senior policy roles in the White House as a special assistant to the president, as a policy advisor to the Senate majority leader, and as a chief of staff to two members of Congress. When the intensity of Bill's jobs became untenable for our family, he went to a large law firm as a corporate consultant for Fortune 500 clients, a job he still has as of this writing. He has a master's degree in political philosophy, and he chairs two nonprofit boards.

We have three adult children launching their own careers. They are amazing people doing exciting things nationally and internationally, and we count ourselves deeply blessed to be their parents.

We said above that Dana's father made some high-risk speculative investments. Well, many years after making one such investment—and a full ten years after his death—one of her dad's big bets finally made good and provided us with a substantial inheritance. This rocked our world because we never aimed at wealth and were consistently making decisions to pursue "missional" work rather than figuring out how to climb the wealth ladder.

For Dana, the inheritance was destabilizing, but for Bill, it was pure joy. We took seriously Jesus's many admonitions about the dangers of wealth, and we set out on a journey to learn from more seasoned Christians how to honor God with our newfound money. That journey led us to multiple organizations and conferences where we heard inspiring stories of generosity and stewardship, many of which you'll read in this book. We've entered an international community of Christians who are passionate about surrendering all their money for the Lord's use. This experience led us to write this book.

We benefited so much from breaking out of the secrecy that usually shrouds money by hearing others' stories, and we want to invite you to bring money out of the shadows of your life so you, too, can find joy in talking about it with fellow Christ-followers and using it as an expression of your love for God. We are inviting you to a carnival, not a funeral, as we encourage you to surrender all you have to the Lord—which is not the same as giving everything away.

We're left-brained, analytical thinkers who thrive in the realm of ideas, but role models are equally important to us because they put flesh on ideas and make them feel real. After Bill wrote his first book, *Dying to Live: Finding Joy in Giving Yourself to God*, our oldest daughter kindly and gently told Bill, "It's good, Dad, but it's not how people learn—people learn through stories." Unfortunately, Bill's book had almost none of those.

This book, however, is chock-full of stories—twenty-four, to be exact. We're blessed to know all the people we interviewed. In each case, we had already heard their story in shorter form over a meal, in a video, or in a small group, and their stories ignited our imagination and inspired us to reshape our lives.

The stories aren't all prescriptive. Many people have made decisions that are unique to God's call on them, so you need not feel guilty if their stories don't match what you believe the Lord is calling you to do. But sometimes we'll hear someone's story and immediately get a sense that "that's got our name on it," and then we do likewise. Such things require prayerful discernment. We hope the stories will inspire you to reflect on how God may be inviting you to steward your resources. In between the stories, you'll get our left-brain analysis.

What Comes Next

As students, we both liked getting a syllabus on the first day of class, showing us what we'd be learning over the semester. So, we'll do that for you here.

First, we'll begin with setting the theological foundation in chapter 1. In chapter 2, we establish that we're stewards, and everything belongs to God. Chapter 3 explores the principles of stewardship that should guide us. In chapter 4, we make the case that God loves multiplication—including nonexploitive and God-honoring profit. We'll examine in chapter 5 why giving *and* investing are both important to the Lord. Chapter 6 lauds the role of work as integral to God's creation and what it means to be human. In chapter 7 we will explore the many dangers of money—what we call a "dangerous blessing." We will get practical about how to steward money in chapter 8, and in chapter 9 we'll examine how God is guiding the church's journey of joy in aligning money with faith. We've also included appendices with a to-do list to start you on your stewardship journey;

books, blogs, podcasts, organizations, and websites that have shaped our understanding of stewardship; and a list summing up what we hope to communicate.

We authored this book together because we are truly one in our love of stewardship. We have a few differences, of course, which we'll note along the way, but our unity far outstrips our disagreements. If you're married, we encourage you to read this book with your spouse. Having a common framework for finances has helped minimize our marital stress, and reading the same books and watching the same videos has been an important part of our unity.

It's worth noting that thirty-five years into our marriage, we still deeply love each other. We complete each other's sentences, we look forward to seeing each other after a long day of work, and we relish just hanging out together. You'll hear bits and pieces about our journey through the book, but we mostly wanted to step out of the way and let you hear others' stories.

Let's start.

Setting the Foundation

Abundance isn't God's provision for me to live in luxury. It's his provision for me to help others live. God entrusts me with his money not to build my kingdom on earth, but to build his kingdom in heaven.

—Randy Alcorn,
Money, Possessions, and Eternity

We're foundational thinkers. We want to understand the philosophical and theological grounding before we work out the implications—bones first, then flesh. Like most people, embodied ideas ignite our imagination, and this first story has been powerful to us for the almost forty years we've known the Bakkes.

Dennis and Eileen Bakke:
Billionaires Cleaning Bathrooms

When we were married in 1989, we began tithing right away because we were committed to giving our firstfruits to the Lord. We trusted that the Lord could prosper us—or not—as He wished. We knew our job was to be faithful.

During our premarital counseling (actually, it was pre-engagement counseling, which we highly recommend since it helps you decide if you should even get engaged), we read Larry Burkett's book *Your Finances in Changing Times*, a biblically grounded book about the basics of financial management. Since couples tend to fight about money, we wanted to minimize conflict by having a common view of finances from the start. And it's worked: We've almost never had a fight about money.

But there was another thing that powerfully shaped our thinking. We had outstanding financial role models in our church on Capitol Hill. Have you ever cleaned church bathrooms with billionaires? We have. Dennis and Eileen Bakke were #129 on *Forbes'* wealthiest people in the United States list with $2 billion,[2] but they pushed our small congregation to have rotating cleaning responsibilities so we could give away a larger percentage of our church budget—and they pulled their weight just like everyone else.

The Bakkes taught adult Sunday school classes about how to honor God with your financial resources, whether vast or limited, and we never missed a class. They modeled for us in word and deed what it meant to be faithful stewards of wealth.

Though Dennis grew up in a family with few financial resources, Eileen said that "Dennis saw his mother write the first check of each month to the church and to missionaries they supported. I grew up in a middle-income family. My parents did not talk about money, but we kids knew they were generous and faithful givers to our church and other community causes." As a young married couple in 1981, Dennis and Eileen set their sights on being good financial stewards before they had much money. They were living in a low-income neighborhood in Washington, DC, when Dennis started his power company, AES Corporation.

From the start of their marriage, Dennis led the way in generosity. Eileen said, "Dennis acknowledged that he was miserly as a kid, but once he had an income, he was so generous to everyone." Dennis believed that AES would be successful, so he started to plan how to structure their giving before the company really took off. Within two years, they started the Mustard Seed Foundation, which has given away over $100 million over forty years. Dennis was never shy about publicly stating his faith in Christ either. In 1997, Dennis told *Forbes*, "Everything we have is not ours, it's the Lord's. We're just stewards of it."[3]

Eileen told us, "Dennis exemplifies radical generosity, not philanthropy. He wants to empower other people, and money is just one way to do that. He doesn't want to build buildings or institutions; he wants to see people thrive." We were recipients of Dennis's and Eileen's love for others, not because we've ever received money from them but because we received their vision of radical generosity. Dennis poured into us—and anyone else who would listen—his vision for using our money as an integral part of following Jesus.

The Bakkes were quick to say that stewardship isn't primarily about what you give away; rather, it's more about what you do with the money you keep. Dennis didn't want to buy a beach house when they could rent one. Same with ski equipment and boats. And fancy cars were unimportant to the couple. Dennis would walk around the house and find things that were no longer being used and say to Eileen, "We need to give this to someone who will use it."

Stewardship isn't primarily about what you give away; rather, it's more about what you do with the money you keep.

It's not that the Bakkes haven't enjoyed the wealth they've been given. "Dennis loves going to nice restaurants and nice hotels, but he has never been defined by being wealthy," Eileen told us. "At heart, he's just a farm boy."

Dennis and Eileen recognized that with wealth comes temptation. To hold themselves accountable, Dennis raised a radical idea with their church small group: share the specifics of their income *and their spending* with their group, even though their fellow group members were not wealthy. Eileen said, "It was very healthy. It represented another layer of trusting God and trusting the people in our lives."

One of the fellow group members asked the Bakkes, "How are you going to keep from increasing your lifestyle as your bank account grows? How will you stay grounded?" Eileen said their friend's challenge was well received because it was given in love and not as a rebuke.

The group also asked, "Do you really need to go somewhere on a private jet?" These weren't leading questions but rather opportunities for the Bakkes to examine their lifestyle with wise, godly friends who love them.

The Bakkes decided many years ago to give away their wealth in their lifetime instead of passing along an endowment for others to manage. In 2023, they wound down the Mustard Seed Foundation, forty years after it began.

After we received an inheritance from Dana's father, we took seriously Jesus's warnings about "the deceitfulness of wealth" (Mark 4:19). So, we asked Dennis a question: "Why is wealth deceitful?"

Without missing a beat, Dennis replied, "It gives you the illusion you're in control, but you're not. God's in control."

Sadly, Dennis is battling dementia and no longer remembers the details of his stewardship journey. Eileen spends her days tenderly caring for Dennis, whom she praises freely more than four decades after they wed. "I love talking about Dennis," she told us.

Dennis may be losing his memory, but the Lord hasn't forgotten him. We relish the thought of the rich welcome he and Eileen will receive from the Lord. They have deeply enriched our lives with their wisdom and godly example of responsible stewardship, and we're indebted to them.

First Principles

The Bakkes live by *first principles*, embodying biblical ideas that bring joy to the world. We also strive to live intentionally, acting in accord with what we say we believe. We love to think "big thoughts" about the world and then seek to implement them in very practical ways. That invites the question, What do we believe? At the foundational level, we believe three things about our financial assets.

First, God owns everything. When we bought our first house with a 10 percent down payment, we used to joke that the only part of the house we truly owned was the powder room—the bank owned the rest of it. In truth, we didn't own any of it. It was all God's. We're stewards of God's stuff, and we'll be called to give account to Him about how we used it. We don't want to hear the words, "I gave you so much, but you were self-indulgent." God's kingdom is eternal, and ours is temporary—but our choices have eternal implications. We yearn to have an abundance . . . in heaven!

Second, God cares about everything. There's nothing about which God is indifferent. Many people put a heavy focus on the Great Commission,[4] but they pay little attention to the Creation Mandate and Cultural Commission.[5] We are meant to flourish in all aspects, bearing fruit and multiplying. The kingdom of God is about more than just saving souls. It's about straightening out the twisted world and striving for the *shalom*, the peace, we knew in the garden of Eden—including in business and financial stewardship.

Third, Jesus taught that we must dethrone money. He proclaimed, "For where your treasure is, there your heart will be also" (Matthew 6:21), and a few verses later, "You cannot serve both God and money." Author Andy Crouch explains that serving money is truly serving a demonic power that wants to have mastery over us in lieu of God.[6] It's an either-or. Living generously is the best way we have discovered to dethrone money in our lives. Generosity has a way of uncoiling the serpent of money from around our hearts.

General Applications

Those are the big ideas that shape our views. Now, let's see those ideas in action, starting with a handful of general applications of a biblical view of money.

Align Our Money with Our Faith

Our faith guides how we use our money, so we strive to bring our money into greater alignment with our faith-based principles and values. To that end, we have changed banks, opened a donor-advised fund,[7] and begun scrutinizing our investments. It's been a step-by-step process, and we're not done yet. We don't want any of our money to be thoughtlessly deployed. It's not been easy, but it's also been fun to see our faith find full expression in all we've been given. It's as though we're expanding our love for God to every corner of our lives.

Engage in Regular Self-Examination

Often, money lies to us and corrupts our hearts and minds. It can lead us to think we're in control of our lives when God wants to be in control. He wants us to put our hope and confidence in Him, not in our bank accounts or our net worth. We know we could lose all we have in a flash.

Money is a dangerous blessing. It can lead us to be greedy, lazy, addicted to luxuries, arrogant, and exploitive. Regular self-examination of how we use money is critical to becoming good stewards.

Seek God's Will in Both Poverty and Plenty

Many people, both inside and outside the church, believe there is something inherently *wrong* with personal wealth. They will see a rich person and assume he's a crook. These people seem to think the call to follow Christ comes with a call to forsake all monetary wealth and live in pious poverty.

But there's nothing inherently good about poverty or inherently bad about wealth. Some people are called to live in poverty, and their obedience is pleasing to the Lord, but it's not necessarily holier than being wealthy. The question is whether we are faithful with what we have, no matter if it's a lot or a little. Our family has experienced both (relative) poverty and wealth, and the challenge to be faithful stewards of whatever God has put in our hands at any time over the years has been the same throughout.

Honor God with Our Hard Work

Work and wealth are closely related. Work pleases God. All work done according to God's will and in His name is holy and sanctifying. We were made to work. Work preceded the fall, and we'll work in heaven.

Work and wealth are closely
related. Work pleases God.
We were made to work.

Our society worships leisure, and many people spend too much time in front of screens. Leisure should be hemmed in. We should rest in order to work, not work in order to rest.

Manage Our Money . . . for the Right Reasons

Radio airwaves and cable television broadcasts are filled with fast-talking "preachers" proclaiming the so-called good news that God wants you to be rich. They say if you're right with God, you'll be flush with cash. If you want to become wealthy, all you have to do is ask God and wait for Him to throw open the storehouses and rain down pennies—and hundred-dollar bills—from heaven.

No.

The health-and-wealth gospel is no gospel at all; it's an oxymoron. We manage, or *steward*, our money because it pleases God. He's given it to us to manage for Him, and we honor Him by our faithful stewardship. But we do not do it just because it's a surefire way to *make* God give us *more*. It isn't.

God calls some to wealth and some to poverty. But our stewardship is a God-given responsibility, not necessarily a way to get rich.

Take Risks

Some people think Christianity is about playing it safe, but we believe God loves seeing His children take risks. Responsible risk helps us flourish. God decides whether that risk will pay off or not. Our job is simply to faithfully follow His call, which certainly includes taking risks. Just ask the disciples and early believers, who risked everything for the sake of the call! (Admittedly, sometimes Bill can take some stupid risks—like riding electric scooters without a helmet in city traffic. It's amazing he's lived to age sixty . . .)

Pray About How to Use and Spend Money

We shouldn't limit our prayer lives to unsaved friends or people's poor health. We should also pray about money—including our investments. God has a plan for each of us, and His plan for you will certainly be different from His call for us. One person can drive a Mercedes in immense joy and in keeping with God's call, while another person's conscience might be burdened by even owning a car. We need to talk to and listen to God to discern His will for us.

Talk About Money

In Western societies, talking about one's money can be like talking about one's underwear—strictly out of bounds in polite conversation! But we believe we should bring our financial details into at least some of our relationships so we can steward our money with accountability. Find some godly friends with whom you can talk specifics about your money. Greed, like mushrooms, grows best in the dark. It's best to bring your money into the light.

Save (But Don't Hoard)

Saving is good, but hoarding is sinful. The Bible is critical both of people who hoard wealth and of people who fail to save for the future. Finding the balance can be tricky, but it can be done. One of Dana's favorite TV shows is *Hoarders*, in part because she has that tendency in herself, and this reminds her of the absurdity of placing too much value in material goods.

Make a Profit

God loves profit. He loves seeing wise investors make a great return by taking a measured risk. Jesus even used this as the basis for a few of His parables. Of course, there are many people who would bristle at the thought. They've been told that profit is wrong, that it means one person took advantage of another. How could God be happy about that?

While God does indeed frown on *dishonest* gain, the Bible never looks down on honest profit. In fact, it is built into creation itself, as we see crops grow after planting or livestock multiplying. The fall has too often twisted profit into exploitation, but it's our job to reclaim profit as God intended it.

By extension, God loves for-profit businesses—and not just to support missionaries. Business can be a powerful agent of God's kingdom, straightening out twisted institutions and customs and bringing hope and joy to the people it serves. Many of the stories in the coming pages will illustrate that beautiful truth.

Sadly, the sacred/secular split has infected our view of money. To God, there is nothing secular—all can be made holy and good (aside from specific activities that He forbids). The idea of a "calling" isn't limited to pastors and missionaries; it includes businesspeople, ballplayers, artists, and architects—and everyone else.

The idea of a "calling" isn't limited to pastors and missionaries; it includes businesspeople, ballplayers, artists, and architects—and everyone else.

It's not just giving that's pleasing to God—so is investing. Both can serve His purposes when they're done for His glory. Here's a crazy thought: pray about your investments, asking the Lord to bless the world through them. Bill prays for our specific investments four times a week. It may sound funny, but God cares about it. If it makes sense for a farmer to pray for a good harvest, why shouldn't God's people pray for their investments?

You're Rich

You may not *feel* wealthy, but most people in the West are, dare we say, *extravagantly* rich—by global standards. That may be a tough pill to swallow, but if we don't recognize our comparative wealth, we are unlikely to understand our corresponding responsibility. Jesus said, "From everyone who has been given much, much will be demanded" (Luke 12:48). Those are sobering words we've framed and hung on our main floor so we won't forget.

Now, what should we be doing in light of this huge responsibility?

Give Generously

At the risk of being legalistic, we're convinced that the tithe should be a floor, not a ceiling. Many of us should be giving more than just 10 percent. Giving our firstfruits means giving to God before giving to Caesar; in other words, pay tithes before taxes. We in the West live in the wealthiest economies in the history of the world, and we should not be trying to give as little as possible!

Live Below Your Means

Lots of books are sold with the promise of imparting financial secrets. Here's one secret that's not complicated but is an absolute superpower: Live below your means and save money. Many people in the West spend as though they expect nothing bad to ever happen to them and therefore live paycheck to paycheck, which is irresponsible and ultimately leads to their dependence on their family or the government to support them. People who are accustomed to living in a wealthy society can learn a lot from people in other parts of the world who are avid savers by necessity because they don't have the government as a safety net.

Looking into Donor-Advised Funds

Donor-advised funds (DAFs)[8] have been awesome for us. In fact, Dana works for one (Impact Foundation). You may not have heard of them, but DAFs are powerful tools to creatively deploy our charitable capital for both grants to nonprofits and investments in for-profit businesses that will hopefully return the capital with interest so it can be granted or reinvested elsewhere. DAFs enable us to increase the impact of our charitable dollars. (We'll explain more in chapter 5.)

Don't Retire Early . . . but Do Take a Break

Brace yourself, because what we're about to say may ruffle your feathers: Don't retire—at least not until it's necessary.

Once you've earned enough so you don't *need* to work anymore, continue working and give away everything you earn. For those of you who are stay-at-home parents whose children have launched, consider joining the paid workforce so you can give that money away. Retirement shouldn't become full-time leisure. And if you do stop working for pay, don't stop working in some capacity. Serve others every day. (More on this in chapter 6.)

Yet don't be a workaholic. Sabbath observance is one excellent way to guard against it. The Lord gave us each of the Ten Commandments for a reason. Our principal identity should not come from our jobs but from Christ. Our society has gone from an overly legalistic observance of the Sabbath in the last century to one that virtually ignores it this century.

Pray Through Financial Decisions

Managing money for God requires a lot of prayer. The question shouldn't only be whether we *can* afford something but whether we *should* afford something. Commit to doing whatever the Lord leads you to do, even if it's hard—and it may not be hard at all. If He's your Lord, then letting Him guide your money only makes sense.

Write It Down

Here's another superpower "secret": Record your spending, giving, saving, and investing. Strive to be intentional about your stewardship. It's easy to deceive ourselves, and regular recordkeeping sheds light on what we *actually* do, not just what we *intend* to do.

Redefine Legacy

Be careful about leaving behind too much money for your children. It's better to leave a legacy of generosity than a huge inheritance. We want to be a blessing to our families after we're gone, but we can bless them by having modeled generosity—to our kids, yes, but also to others. Think carefully about how much of your wealth should be bequeathed to your children.

Set Goals

Set giving goals. Try to subvert acquisitive tendencies by channeling them into generosity. Dream about more than vacations—dream about ways to lift people out of poverty or to plant churches among the unreached. We have some audacious giving goals that we don't yet see a path to reach, but striving for them helps to keep us from becoming endless consumers.

Avoid Consumer Debt

We made it our goal to be debt-free (which we are), even if it might make more financial sense to carry low-interest loans. There is enormous freedom in owing nothing. Dana felt liberated when we paid off our mortgage.

The list above feels like our version of Luther's Ninety-Five Theses nailed to the church door in Wittenberg: Here we stand, we can do no other! But, of course, we're also on a learning journey, and in time we might add or subtract from our principles or change how we express them. We've learned much about stewardship in the last thirty-five years, and we are eager to keep learning.

Our adult children tease us about how much we talked about money and stewardship when they were growing up, and it's true that we love the topic! Although we focus on financial stewardship in this book, we're also zealous about using our time, talent, and ties (relationships) for God. We find enormous joy in talking about how to live out our faith in Christ with all our resources, including our money.

> Although we focus on financial stewardship in this book, we're also zealous about using our time, talent, and ties (relationships) for God.

April and Craig Chapman: Premeditated Giving

Each of the stories in the book has helped shape our stewardship journey, but several have been especially precious to us. The Bakkes' story was first because of how it influenced us as twentysomethings. The Chapmans' story has been important because we've been so privileged to learn from our "older siblings" in stewardship (though we're about the same age).

April and Craig Chapman grew up in families that taught that security began with financial independence. Generosity was not modeled for them. When Craig first heard about a group called Generous Giving, he said, "Man, I am not getting involved in that organization— they're going to make me feel guilty about what I'm *not* giving away!"

But the Lord began working in them in the first year of their marriage. "We were impressed by Malachi 3:8, which essentially says that 'You're robbing from me by not bringing in my tithes and offerings. Test me and see if you won't have overflowing blessings.' We liked the sound of that, and we began tithing 10 percent even though we both had a lot of debt."

Step One: Tithe

The Chapmans, software engineers at Microsoft, had a growing desire to lean into generosity and give away more of their money to further the gospel. But Craig lamented, "We felt that, as technology geeks, we couldn't serve the Lord as well as if we had careers in a field like medicine."

At a Christian conference in 1999, April and Craig— who today are still just as affectionate as high school sweethearts, even though they've been married thirty-one years—were walking hand in hand around a beautiful lake at the foot of the Rocky Mountains. As they talked, they learned that the Lord had spoken to each of them independently the night before that He was about to use them in new and exciting ways to serve the kingdom, and it would involve leaving their comfortable positions at Microsoft. April told us that it was as though God was just starting to open the curtain on a theater stage: "We had a sense of anticipation and excitement."

Step Two: Dream Bigger Than Tithing 10 Percent

"We were hooked on this joy of giving obediently, but we wanted to give more of our lives," April said. She and Craig were introduced to the acronym of LIFE—Labor, Influence, Finances, and Expertise—and began to think about how to look beyond just financial giving. April decided to leave Microsoft and start a consulting firm to develop Internet strategies for Christian nonprofits. Craig followed a few years later, devoting his time to volunteering while they lived on stock options they had earned.

Step Three: Give More Than Money

A fellow Microsoft veteran asked Craig to help him start a tech company. Initially, Craig declined, thinking that his new mission in life was empowering nonprofits with his time and expertise.

However, one morning, while reflecting on Romans 12:2 about being transformed by the renewing of his mind, Craig experienced a shift in perspective. He realized that his identity was no longer tied to his job but was instead rooted in Christ. He felt the Lord calling him to live out this identity through the company he would help create, and a significant part of that calling was to give away half of his equity in the company. This was an opportunity to give from all four parts of the LIFE model, using his labor, influence, finances, and expertise for the Lord's work.

Within minutes of hearing God's voice through this message, the phone rang, and Craig's future business partner said he had to know that day whether Craig would join him—and his answer was easy: "I'm in!"

The company was remarkably successful, far beyond what Craig ever imagined. After seven years, he decided to leave the company and sell a significant amount of his shares. True to the Lord's call, Craig gifted half of his distribution to their donor-advised fund at National Christian Foundation. The Chapmans were experiencing incredible joy in their giving and were increasingly excited about giving more.

Step Four: Follow Through on Your Commitments

Next, the Chapmans made a strategic decision to not disburse their DAF quickly but rather invest it and grow it over time. They still made many outright grants, but they also made impact investments that returned profits to the DAF to create an economic engine that enabled them to give more. Consequently, they've been able to give away more than their original contribution and have created a giving flywheel for future grants and investments.

Step Five: Wisely Steward Your Giving to Maximize Impact over the Long Term[9]

From their first year of marriage, the Lord was "slowly revealing to us more about His heart for giving and investing. It's still unfolding more than thirty years later," Craig told us. And what came next was significant: The Lord led the Chapmans to think about how their money was invested, not just to whom it was given. They began investing for impact, aligning their capital with their faith, both inside their donor-advised fund and in their private investments. They began working with Christian entrepreneurs who were seeking to advance kingdom principles through their businesses.

Step Six: Use ALL Your Money to Advance the Kingdom (Not Just Your Charitable Dollars)

Today, the Chapmans' journey continues. April told us, "I feel like the Lord is always equipping us for the next thing, and we've come to depend on that. We've found that if we seek, listen, and act on what the Lord tells us, it's an amazing adventure." They discovered that living generously with their finances has fueled generosity and joy in all the other areas of their LIFE.

Love for the Lord wafts out of all the Chapmans say and do. They are the aroma of Christ to us—they're our heroes and role models, and we're blessed and honored to hear the voice of God through them on so many occasions. We regularly share with them very personally and specifically about every facet of our finances so they can guide us in our own growth in stewardship.

The Chapmans' fondest wish? "At the end of our days, we'd love it if the Lord would say, 'Craig and April served my purposes in their generation.'"

Of that, we have no doubt.

Oh, and that Generous Giving group Craig wanted nothing to do with all those years ago? April is now the CEO!

The Bakkes and the Chapmans have, by their examples, helped us pour the theological foundation of our finances. They've lived out their convictions that God owns everything, cares about everything, and that He alone must sit enthroned in our hearts. When money is put in its rightful place under God's authority, we will be equipped to align all our financial resources with our faith, intentionally leaning into generosity and faith-driven investing, being wary of consumer debt, saving for the unexpected, and carefully managing our money to the glory of God. Holy living entails all our money.

In chapter 2, we'll explore what it means to steward God's resources.

Everything Belongs to God

Every faculty you have, your power of thinking or of moving your limbs from moment to moment, is given you by God. If you devoted every moment of your whole life exclusively to His service you could not give Him anything that was not in a sense His own already. . . . It is like a small child going to its father and saying, "Daddy, give me sixpence to buy you a birthday present." It is all very nice and proper, but only an idiot would think that the father is sixpence to the good on the transaction.

—C. S. Lewis, *Mere Christianity*

[Jesus answered,] "Go, sell your possessions and give to the poor, and you will have treasure in heaven. Then come, follow me." When the young man heard this, he went away sad, because he had great wealth.

—Matthew 19:21–22

Allie Eberle: Trading the High Life for the Slums

Allie Eberle (née Amoroso) sat on the beach beneath the Golden Gate Bridge. As she watched the sunset on a late July evening in 2018, she wondered if God was calling her to make a bold move for His kingdom that would befuddle the world. Her luxury apartment was just a stone's throw away, and her employer's high-rise office was nearby. She was considering giving it all up for a Kenyan slum.

Allie's meetings for the day had been unexpectedly canceled, allowing her to freely follow the advice of her spiritual mentor, who told her to take three days to wrestle with God.

Growing up in a wealthy suburb of Washington, DC, her life was the stuff of dreams.

She'd been striving for years to get where she was: a fast-track job with a bright future. A straight-A student in high school, she was accepted to study at the University of Virginia, where she excelled. Allie then outpaced her peers, arriving in Silicon Valley and ascending quickly in a Fortune 100 company. The opportunities were limitless, and Allie was eager to chase them.

The problem was God's plans were interfering with Allie's. Ten months earlier, as she recovered from a car accident, she had knelt on her bed and read the Bible. Allie felt the voice of God in her spirit saying, "Go back!" Allie immediately knew where: Mathare, the Nairobi slum where half a million people live in two square miles of raw sewage, garbage, and squalor.

Allie first saw Nairobi in college when she studied abroad in Kenya for a semester. She heard the young women who lived in Mathare relate the abuse, rape, and murder that scarred their lives. Allie returned to school and to her partying ways that were a spiritual slum, but she couldn't quite shake what she had witnessed. She remembered talking to a distraught young woman—twenty-one years old, just as Allie had been—who explained that her husband had left her and their three kids that very day, forcing them to fend for themselves in their dirt-floored shack. Allie also remembered the day someone assaulted her while attempting to steal her gold cross necklace. This place was dangerous.

The thought of leaving her comfortable life and luminous professional future for the seeming hopelessness of Mathare was scary. But God had been teaching her that she wasn't on her own—and that everything belonged to Him.

Allie was lonely in San Francisco and eager for human connection. She saw a crowd of twentysomethings filing into a theater one day and decided to follow them in. As it turned out, a church was using the theater for services. Sitting in the front row, Allie said, "Week after week, I cried away my sin." But still, she said, "I wasn't completely surrendered to God."

God, however, kept pursuing Allie. One day, she met with a private equity investor in Los Gatos, California, named Henry Kaestner (whose story is in chapter 9). Her goal was cultivating an investor for her work, but God's goal was cultivating her heart for *His* work. Henry—a devout

Christ-follower, accomplished entrepreneur, and start-up expert—didn't want to hear Allie's deal pitches . . . but he was keen to learn more about Allie's experience in Kenya.

"He wanted to know why I cared about Kenya and how business and entrepreneurship could change the lives of people living in Mathare," she recalled. "This was the first time I saw that you can work for God through business."

By the end of the meeting, "Henry laid hands on me and prayed for me in that mom-and-pop coffee shop. That was a turning point—to see how I could combine my love of entrepreneurship with faith in Christ."

But Allie was still holding something back. She was afraid of what people—including her parents—would think if she abandoned her impressive career to focus on a forsaken slum so far away.

Months after that providential coffee with Henry, Allie was at an inflection point on the beach as she scanned the San Francisco sunset. "It's then that I just turned my hands over and said, 'Take my life and use it for Your good. I surrender everything to You.' And I knew then that I was going to quit my job and move to Kenya."

With that decision, Allie turned her back on immense wealth, prestige, and safety. Within a matter of months and at age twenty-three, Allie founded ROSE (Restoration of Sisters in the Extreme) Women's Foundation. ROSE teaches women in Kenya how to triple their annual income through biblically based training on bookkeeping, market-ing, management, and essential business skills. Instead of using her brilliance in California's Big Tech industry, Allie let God show her where and how He wanted to display her gifts—making a massive difference in Mathare.

We visited Allie in February 2023 and sat in the back of a darkened shack (the power was out again) that featured a ceiling made of blue vinyl tarp. A lady spoke in Swahili as thirty-five other women, some with toddlers clinging to their legs, intently listened as they were instructed on the basics of spreadsheets. This was why we came: to see the power of entrepreneurship unleashed in the lives of these impoverished women. This was the very tangible expression of "teaching a person to fish." In that stuffy, crowded room, human ingenuity was being liberated.

Would these women soon be living in air-conditioned houses with a new car parked out front? Hardly. Allie explains, "Poverty alleviation looks a lot different than what we would imagine in the West. A woman who lived with a dirt floor and corrugated roof is now living in the same neighborhood but in a brick building in one room with a shared bathroom for fifty people and a door that can lock. But that is a huge step up in her dignity, in her ability to provide for her family. Her life is drastically different, but it may not look that way to many Americans."

Allie beams with joy as she explains how women in Mathare are empowered by the ROSE Women's Foundation. Though a Christian organization, ROSE serves women of all faiths and is well on its way to reaching thousands a year.

If Allie thought she owned her multiple gifts and talents, she might have made different choices. Instead, she believes that God owns everything. Allie's goal is to use what God has given her to please the Lord.

Not Yours to Own

Allie's story reminds us of what the apostle Paul wrote to the church in Corinth: "What do you have that you did not receive? And if you did receive it, why do you boast as though you did not?" (1 Corinthians 4:7). Everything we have is a gift of God.

Once we recognize that we are stewards and not owners, we begin measuring our lives by what the true owner thinks. If God has loaned you a set of gifts, skills, and opportunities to be used to please Him, then you'll make decisions based on that reality. This mindset is foreign to people who see themselves as autonomous beings beholden to no one.

Once we recognize that we are stewards and not owners, we begin measuring our lives by what the true owner thinks.

Bill:

My father, Bob, was a grateful man who knew he belonged to God. He loved the Lord and regularly acknowledged that his successes in life were attributable to God first and foremost. He seemed to go through life continually amazed at how much he had been given rather than what he lacked. He wasn't wealthy, but you would have thought he was the richest man in the world by the way he talked. It wasn't that he led a charmed life either. He lost his beloved wife of fifty-four years (and my mother) to a sudden heart attack and lived alone the last nine years of his life. Like many men of his generation, he had never learned to cook or do laundry, but he quickly taught himself everything he needed to know. In a short time, he was preparing home-cooked meals and hosting dinner parties at his apartment. His gaze was fixed on what he had—and Who had him. He acknowledged God's owner-ship of his many gifts, and it allowed him to dwell in almost continuous contentment.

My dad would often talk about his many blessings, includ-ing his success as an industrial chemical salesman, and he always thanked God. One of his good friends, who was not a Christ-follower, rebuked him for what he thought was a mis-attribution. "Oh, Bob," he said, "it's not because of God that you're successful. You did this!" Dad didn't buy it for a second. He knew it was all from the Lord.

Americans celebrate people who pull themselves up by their own bootstraps—"self-made" men and women. There's a sense that people who make it on their own are heroic. In one sense, that is noble. Hard work, thrift, and diligence are laudable. But no one *truly* makes it on their own. All of us can trace our successes to other people and circumstances. We are inherently dependent creatures, and failing to recognize the gifts we've received from others is prideful, not praiseworthy.

The fundamental sin of the garden was pride. Adam and Eve succumbed to the serpent's lie that God doesn't know what's best for us; they took matters into their own hands so they could become like God in knowing good and evil. The prohibition against eating the one fruit in the middle of the garden could just as well have been some other prohibition. The core issue was not the fruit but distrusting God's wisdom. Instead, they arrogated to themselves that which belongs to God alone.

What do you have that you haven't been given by God? Your height, your skin, your facial features, your brain's chemical balance, and your genes are all inherited. The same is true with your lineage. You didn't get to choose your parents, where you were born, when you were born—none of it. Much of who you are today comes from circumstances out of your control.

Do you ever wonder whether there are people who would have been world-class pianists and artists and orators and surgeons and university presidents who are instead slave laborers making bricks so they can feed their families? Thanks to Allie's work, though, perhaps a woman in Mathare will eventually ascend to work for—or even run—a successful international company. By the "accident" of where and to whom they were born, some people will attain enduring fame. Others will die in obscurity with dirt under their nails.

Far from causing despair, humbly acknowledging this truth reminds us that we own nothing. But just because we own nothing doesn't mean we *are* nothing. We are loved by our Creator, the Giver whose presence is the ultimate gift.

And He calls us to steward the gifts He has bestowed on us. Like Abraham, God blesses us so that we may bless others (Genesis 12:2–3).

> But just because we own nothing
> doesn't mean we *are* nothing.

Can't I Take Credit for Some Things?

By now you might be thinking, *Yes, some things are beyond my control. They're inherited gifts. But I've cultivated those gifts through arduous work and hours of self-denying practice. And I've taken some of my weaknesses and worked on them tirelessly to the point that I can now say they're strengths.* Fair point.

Bill:

I love racquetball. It's just below my love of God and family. I practice a lot, watch instructional videos, and even took private lessons. I keep threatening to give notice at my day job as soon as a major sports brand sponsors me to go pro! But my backhand used to stink—until I practiced it thousands of times to the point that people now comment on how good it is. Through time and hard work, I turned a weakness into a strength.

Dana:

I used to be very disorganized. But I read books and watched videos about organization. Today, you can open any cabinet in our house and see hyper-organization with folders, labels, and bins. I turned a weakness into a strength.

Surely, we can take credit for these successes as our own, right? Where did we get the time to turn our weaknesses into strengths? And the tenacity? And the equipment? And the role models? These were all gifts given to us. Certainly, God gives us agency to make good choices, but we should remember how even our good choices are undergirded by God's blessings.

Like most people, Dana has a wide span of moods and emotions. Bill, on the other hand, has two moods: happy and very happy. Bill wakes up happy and goes to sleep happy. It's easy for him to think he's happy because he's more virtuous than others, following in his father's footsteps by giving thanks regularly and focusing on what he has instead of what he lacks. Yet a 2005 study found that 50 percent of our happiness is determined by our genes, 40 percent by our activities, and 10 percent by our life circumstances.[10] If that's correct, where is there room for self-congratulation?

Deuteronomy 8:17–18 captures it well: "You may say to yourself, 'My power and the strength of my hands have produced this wealth for me.' But remember the LORD your God, for it is he who gives you the ability to produce wealth, and so confirms his covenant, which he swore to your ancestors, as it is today."

Suzanne Daniel: A Heart of Generosity

People who are born into wealth may have an advantage in understanding that no one truly makes it on their own, but they must still come to "own" the responsibility of steward-ing wisely. Suzanne Daniel has done just that.

"I remember when I was in elementary school, and a bus stop friend whose parents had just divorced told me her mom couldn't afford to buy her a coat," Suzanne told us. "I talked to my dad about it, and we agreed to put an envelope of money under their doormat on Christmas Eve. They never found out who gave them the money, which is the way my dad taught me to give."

Suzanne, now in her fifties, has been giving away money ever since. The spirit of generosity runs deep in her, and not just financially. Early in her life, she noticed the road leading into her neighborhood was strewn with trash, which deeply bothered Suzanne. As a second grader, she organized a neighborhood trash pickup and was surprised to see the work featured in the local newspaper.

In middle school, Suzanne was volunteering at a vet-erinary hospital, and she regularly saw people who had to choose between paying their rent or caring for their sick or injured animals. One person had a beautiful horse that would be euthanized unless they could produce the money for eye surgery. Suzanne convinced her father to pay for the surgery. To manage Suzanne's endless pleas for charity, her father put her on a giving budget.

Four decades later, Suzanne still struggles to live within a giving budget, but now it's in the millions of dollars since she took over her father's family foundation—capitalized by money he earned as an extraordinarily successful mutual fund manager. As an inheritor of wealth, Suzanne equates her position to the experience of her Christian faith. She did nothing to earn it—neither her salvation nor the money; she is only a steward of what has been shared with her. "It's all the Lord's, and I ask every day for wisdom to deploy it well. I hope all our resources provide life and hope to others and a chance to hear about how much Jesus loves them," Suzanne said.

Her heart for the international poor began when she took a mission trip to a Haitian orphanage. "That trip totally changed me," she told us. "Holding on my lap this impoverished child the same age as my nine-year-old son was just too much for me. I ran outside to the truck and wept." That deep sorrow led Suzanne to find ways to support families in poverty to prevent child abandonment.

Suzanne's passion to lift up the world's poor has sent her and her veterinarian husband, Marc, and their four kids to developing countries the world over. We recently visited Allie Eberle's ministry in Nairobi's Mathare slum with Suzanne and Marc.

Suzanne readily concedes that "being a grant maker for twenty-six years could easily give you a hero complex. Even if you're not asking that your name be put on the side of a building, there's a power differential between me and the person receiving the funds that I don't feel comfortable with."

Suzanne's day job running the foundation has taken an unexpected turn in recent years. Instead of solely giving away money, the foundation is now investing a sizable portion of its endowment in faith-driven entrepreneurs in frontier markets like Kenya. Investing isn't just another way to make money so the foundation can give out more grants; it's become core to the mission. (You'll read more about investing your charitable capital in chapter 4.)

The shift in focus from grant-making to investing in entrepreneurship began when Suzanne met Julie Colombino-Billingham, a first-generation Italian American who had been a professional dancer and aerial acrobat before earning her MBA. Julie, who was ministering to the poor of Port-au-Prince, quickly realized that the women she was seeking to help needed jobs more than they needed charity. Julie responded by founding Deux Mains, a solar-powered business that produces high fashion handbags and accessories. During a visit to Haiti, Suzanne heard Julie speak at the grand opening of the factory and plaintively asked her, "How are you funding this? Do you need investments? How can we invest in Deux Mains?" Neither Julie nor Suzanne knew how to do that, which led Suzanne to seek out Aimee Minnich at Impact Foundation (see Aimee's story in chapter 5). Aimee coached Suzanne and Julie, and today Suzanne's foundation is investing significant resources in profitable businesses worldwide that provide good jobs that transform lives.

The investing side of running the foundation doesn't come naturally to Suzanne. "I'm the least likely person in the room when it comes to finances. My father was a wizard at it, but it's hard work for me—and humbling, which is a good thing. I don't like spreadsheets or the financial world, but I'm excited to see the impact."

An analysis of her foundation's investments by an outside consultant revealed a disturbing set of facts: They were invested in dozens of companies whose products, services, and values were antithetical to the foundation's mission. What the foundation's grants were trying to achieve was being counteracted by the funds generating the grants— like the left hand and the right hand were working against one another. "We had dirty money coming in that was feeding grants to worthy causes," Suzanne said.

The fund managers at the foundation didn't initially see eye to eye with Suzanne. "I felt like I was this rainbows-and-unicorns-do-gooder arguing for a double bottom line," Suzanne told us. In time, the trustees have come to see the value in using the endowment for more than just a money-making machine to do grant-making. They've come to see it's possible to do good while doing well.

Suzanne is now so busy helping to manage the endowment through impact investing that she is turning over some of her grant-making responsibilities to others—a hard decision for someone who loves seeing the world transformed through giving. "But it feels like a calling to me, and I need to be obedient," Suzanne told us. And she's just as involved—if not more involved—in transforming lives through stewarding the endowment, which is much larger than the annual grants.

That same little girl who persuaded her father to put money under her neighbor's doormat and had to be put on a giving budget has matured in her efforts to help those in need. Today, she's a seasoned investor/giver leaning into more holistic ways to empower the powerless and prevent poverty from being the narrative for thousands of people.

Confidence: Owned or Given?

Suzanne's story demonstrates the importance of remembering God is the first giver and we only emulate His generosity. And there's another gift that we are tempted to call our own: self-confidence.

Think of that activity in which you excel and how confident you can feel in it. You might recognize your many weaknesses, but in that one strength you feel like you'll never falter. Perhaps you can hear a complex concept and summarize it pithily (Bill is good at this). Or maybe you can examine a problem that seems opaque to others and then provide an outside-the-box solution (Dana is good at this). Whatever it is, there's probably something that you've been good at your whole life, and you can't imagine ever being weak in that area. That gives you confidence.

But confidence is a gift that can suddenly change. Think of the star athlete who is paralyzed by an injury. Or the historian whose dementia destroys their ability to recall past events with remarkable detail. The point is this: We have no room for confidence about our futures.

The oldest book in the Bible describes a confident man named Job who had everything going for him: health, wealth, family, faith, and prestige. But Satan complains that Job's faith in God is only because of the blessings God has handed him: Remove the blessings, and Job's trust in the Lord would also depart. God grants Satan permission to test Job. He becomes impoverished, desperately sick, and mired in constant pain. He loses his children, and his wife tells him to "curse God and die" (Job 2:9). Pretty horrible. Job doesn't curse God, but his faith is near collapse as he accuses God of being unfair. Job's confidence was shot to pieces.

We should be confident in God's love, not our own gifts that can be taken away at any time. Gifts are not meant to puff us up with self-confidence; they are meant to remind us that all praise belongs to the Giver.

No Credit and No Blame?

But if we don't own anything, if it's all a gift from God, then how can we be held responsible? If we can't take credit, do we also avoid all blame?

We may not own anything, but God owns us. And He commands us to be good stewards of what He has entrusted to us. The Bible teaches us that "every good and perfect gift is from above" (James 1:17) *and* that if we're faithful with a little we'll be given more (Matthew 25:14–30). Both things are true. We live in gratitude for what we've been given, and we faithfully steward it for God's glory. We know we can't earn God's salvation, but we can earn His pleasure. God is easily pleased but impossible to satisfy—meaning we can't get into heaven on our own merit, but the kind of reception we receive is partially dependent on our faithfulness in this life. We don't want to be one who "shrinks back" (Hebrews 10:38). As stewards, we lean on Him for the wisdom and strength to know how to properly handle the many gifts and responsibilities we've been given.

> As stewards, we lean on Him for the wisdom and strength to know how to properly handle the many gifts and responsibilities we've been given.

It's customary to talk about our lives as gifts from God. But we see our lives principally as responsibilities that we've been given to steward. If returned to God as living sacrifices, our existence can be a gift to others. But being a living sacrifice—which is the phrase Paul uses in Romans 12:1—doesn't come naturally to humans. Born in sin, our natural inclination is to own our lives. We've fallen in the past, and we're likely to fall in the future. We're weak, near-sighted, and quick to forget. We are like Peter, who in a few hours went from vigorously insisting he'd never deny Jesus to thrice swearing he never knew Him.

But Jesus did something else. In the garden of Gethsemane, He submitted to the Father's will. It was a bitter cup that Jesus earnestly asked to be spared from drinking, but He quickly added, "Not as I will, but as you will" (Matthew 26:39). That's arguably the most important quotation in all human history. If Jesus had not accepted His Father's will, we'd be in a world of hurt. There would be no hope beyond the grave; all we'd have is the good creation, then the fall, and then despair. Instead, Jesus allowed the very people He was saving to nail Him to the cross. In that act of submission, the sins of all people for all time were fully paid for. And His resurrection on the third day proved that He had defeated sin, death, and the devil.

We look to Jesus as the perfect example of stewardship. Our lives are responsibilities to be poured out for others. That should make us more attentive to God's will for us. We dare not be among those who start well and finish poorly.

We are always afraid we'll mess up. Anytime we think we've got this faithful life thing figured out, we're in trouble. Paul wrote to the Corinthians, "If you think you are standing firm, be careful that you don't fall!" (1 Corinthians 10:12). But God is always with us, and He will show us the way if we only surrender to His will and steward His gifts—just as the Larsons do.

Don and Terri Larson: From Comfort to Courage

Don Larson was in his boxer shorts when he heard his wife, Terri, frantically yelling for him from the driveway of their Mozambique home in the middle of the night. Don grabbed his nunchucks and stun gun and ran outside. A Mozambican man greeted him by pointing an AK-47 at Don's chest and screaming obscenities. Don dropped his weapons, was shoved back inside the house, and was told to quickly find the keys to both his cars. A second gunman was pointing his weapon at Terri and their sons as they knelt outside.

"I can't find my keys," Don yelled to Terri. Terri yelled back, "Don, I've told you a million times to put the keys in the same place every time!" As Don thought he was in the final minutes of his life, that was the last thing he wanted to hear!

The gunman counted down, "Three! Two! One!" Thankfully, he kept restarting the count as Don scrambled for the keys. He finally found them, and the gunmen drove off with both cars, never to be seen again.

Two years earlier, Don Larson had been living the good life in southeastern Pennsylvania. As a Hershey Company executive, he had a large house with a swimming pool. He drove a Porsche, his three kids were in private schools, and Don flew his own hot air balloon. Don and Terri were living the American Dream until the Lord opened his eyes and got ahold of his heart.

After leaving Hershey, he became the CEO of a cocoa processing company and traveled to African countries where he saw devastating poverty. "I was shocked by what I saw. That trip changed my life." When his company was acquired, he had many other employment opportunities. But he was led to pray about what's next, submitting his will to God's. And the Lord had a wild idea in mind: Sell everything and move your family to Mozambique to start a cashew company. Talk about a curveball! And here's the thing: Don and Terri did exactly what the Lord told them to do. They've now been in Mozambique for twelve years and own a thriving cashew processing plant in Matola.

"I don't just want to help people get by," Don says. "I want to pull them out of poverty."

A few years ago, when pondering our next family vacation, Dana had the idea to visit the Larsons. We had

learned about their story through a TEDx talk, and we had
met Don for coffee in the DC area when he was here for
meetings. But we didn't know him well, and it was slightly
strange for us to travel halfway around the world to stay in
his home. The night before we arrived, we worried that we
were doing something crazy. Who are these people?

We found out: They're the real deal. They live in a modest home with power that comes and goes, unreliable Internet service, and poverty all around them. The city roads
make you feel seasick because they're littered with huge
potholes, and the problem is even worse in the countryside.
But the Larsons are happy. Sure, they miss the cozy life they
had in Pennsylvania, but the sense of purpose and meaning
that saturates their business makes it all worthwhile. That
one factory, which sells cashews worldwide, has a multiplying effect providing good jobs: fifty factory workers, one
thousand workers to shell the cashews, and fifty thousand
farming families to grow them.

Why would Don and Terri move to Mozambique?
Because they know they're stewards, not owners, of what
God has given them. If they were owners and never had to
answer to God or anyone else, they might not have made
the radical choices they did.

Is it fear of an angry God that drives them? No, it's
love for a generous God who invites us to join with Him in
mending a broken world, loving others, and helping people
flourish.

It's often said that "you can't take it with you" but
"you can send it ahead." By expending themselves and
their resources on behalf of the least of these in one of the

poorest countries in the world, Don and Terri are storing up treasures in heaven that are not susceptible to market downturns or theft. They know they have gifts, skills, and abilities that come from God, and they are creatively employing them on behalf of former strangers—because they want to please God. They're taking the five talents God gave them and multiplying them many times over.

God owns us—all of us—whether we recognize it or not. We can't own anything in our lives except our sin. Even our confidence is a gift that can vanish in a moment. God created us and gave us gifts, but it is our responsibility to use them how He wants. Allie Eberle, Suzanne Daniel, and the Larsons have heeded this call.

Having established that we're stewards, we'll turn to the principles that should guide our stewardship.

The Implications of Stewardship

A lot of people accuse me of being generous. And that's because I know whose money it is. It's the Lord's money. It's not mine. Because if it were mine, none of you would be getting one red cent of it.

—Foster Friess, philanthropist
September 13, 2007, at a Men of Faith
Breakfast speech, Denver, Colorado

Kate Gardner: Trust Fund Kid Done Good

"Trust Fund Kid" usually connotes being privileged, spoiled, and self-indulgent. That doesn't describe Kate Gardner.

Kate told us:

On the morning of my twenty-first birthday, my parents took me out to a restaurant. To my utter surprise, they told me that I would be given a sizable investment portfolio, with full access. My grandfather had done something similar for my father, to great success, and now my dad wanted to continue the family tradition with me. I couldn't believe it. "This is something we want you to have for the rest of your life with a long-term growth mindset," my dad told me. They made it clear that they wanted me to take ownership of these resources, but they were ready to walk with me as I learned to use it well.

Kate's parents had grown a business into a powerhouse financial firm. Her father's inheritance narrative had led to his exploration of and keen knack for investing—and now, it was his turn to pass on the resources. "They had been preparing me for this by their wise examples for my whole life," Kate said. "And they trusted me and believed in me and the gifts the Lord gave me."

Kate views her inherited wealth the same way she sees her salvation—as a gift from God that she doesn't deserve but that she's responsible to steward faithfully. She resonates with fellow Princeton alumnus Frederick Buechner, who wrote in his book *Wishful Thinking*, "The place God calls you to is the place where your deep gladness and the world's deep hunger meet."[11]

Kate's deep gladness comes from encouraging others. "I love to be a cheerleader for people in their callings. In terms of the 'world's hunger,' it seems to me that missions work, in the spreading of the gospel, would be at the core."

Upon receiving her sizable inheritance, Kate gave away 30 percent in a "tithe" of sorts, introducing her to the joy of giving. With careful investing, she's been able to continue giving away large sums each year, leaning into the wise financial stewardship her parents had believed she would exhibit.

Kate has combined her gift of encouragement with her gift of wealth. Rather than working for pay when she has no need for more money, Kate spends her days in intentional and deep encouragement of others. At one point, she was keeping notes on over six hundred people to be able to keep up with their lives and pray for them. She was having on average ten daily video calls with those she supports around the world. She has now gone deeper in mentorship with a smaller group of women and also supports the work of about sixty missionaries in more than twenty nations. She doesn't just write a check; she seeks to engage in purposeful conversations and pray with them.

"When I contribute to a missionary, I'm also looking for a relationship so I can be a cheerleader for their work. Finances are just part of my investment in them. Spiritual, relational, and financial investment—I want to make all three," Kate told us. With a dynamic personality and seemingly limitless energy, Kate deploys all of her being to encourage others. She's personable, enthusiastic, and kind, and she talks to you with a twinkle in her eye with love exuding from her countenance. It's palpable.

Kate also leans into investing her capital in businesses with a double bottom line: spiritual and financial. She's come to understand the key role for-profit business can play in addressing global problems. Just as she does with the missionaries she supports, Kate loves praying with and for the entrepreneurs in whose work she's invested.

She doesn't deploy any of her capital without her "creative forms of generosity" in stewarding prayer and community building—"something very close to my heart," she said.

Financial stewardship necessarily connects to what we love. Kate says, "My dad taught me that the root word of *invest* in Latin is *investire*—the same word that is the root of a priest's vestments. True investing is like putting on the vestments of the company, like putting on the jersey of your favorite sports team. My dad has a personal saying on his company's office wall—'Make your portfolio reflect your best vision of our future.' I like to think about this in giving and ministry as well—the portfolio of our lives reflecting the vision of God's kingdom come."

Kate doesn't shy away from talking about her wealth precisely because she doesn't believe it's hers—it belongs to the Lord, and she's just a steward. This openness also has its pitfalls. Kate hates to see the confusion and disappointment in the eyes of those whose good work she can't support financially. She's also experienced people seeking to sidle up to her precisely because of her wealth, sometimes seeking to take advantage of her generosity. "There are burdens that come with blessing," Kate said. "It's complex. I've found that the best way to navigate stewardship is in community with other people."

Kate is eager to talk about money precisely because she knows that with financial resources comes great responsibility. She has hosted a podcast called *Ascendants*, directed to inheritors of great wealth, and she's writing a book. She's not proud about her wealth, both because she didn't earn it and because she knows she will be asked to give an account to the Lord for how she used her talents.

Kate's story is the mirror opposite of the prodigal son's or the rich young ruler's: She's passionate about using everything she's been given—her time, talent, treasure, and ties—to the praise and glory of God.

Why Do We Steward?

Kate has fixed in her mind that everything belongs to the Lord. She sees herself as a steward of God's resources, not as an owner.

Living in light of the reality that we will have to answer for our choices changes our perspective. In the Wichterman household, our kids often heard us opine on death—theirs and ours. We believe that there's no good that comes from avoiding the topic and much good that comes from focusing on it. Hardly a day passes that we don't think about the fact that the human condition is terminal, and we will soon be forgotten by just about everyone—except God and those with whom we will spend eternity. That ever-present reality helps shape the here and now, making us more grateful for what we have and more intent on preparing to meet God.

Luke's Gospel records Jesus's story about a man who lived only for this life:

> There was a rich man who was dressed in purple and fine linen and lived in luxury every day. At his gate was laid a beggar named Lazarus, covered with sores and

longing to eat what fell from the rich man's table. Even the dogs came and licked his sores.

The time came when the beggar died and the angels carried him to Abraham's side. The rich man also died and was buried. In Hades, where he was in torment, he looked up and saw Abraham far away, with Lazarus by his side. So he called to him, "Father Abraham, have pity on me and send Lazarus to dip the tip of his finger in water and cool my tongue, because I am in agony in this fire."

But Abraham replied, "Son, remember that in your lifetime you received your good things, while Lazarus received bad things, but now he is comforted here and you are in agony. And besides all this, between us and you a great chasm has been set in place, so that those who want to go from here to you cannot, nor can anyone cross over from there to us."

He answered, "Then I beg you, father, send Lazarus to my family, for I have five brothers. Let him warn them, so that they will not also come to this place of torment."

Abraham replied, "They have Moses and the Prophets; let them listen to them."

"No, father Abraham," he said, "but if someone from the dead goes to them, they will repent."

He said to him, "If they do not listen to Moses and the Prophets, they will not be convinced even if someone rises from the dead." (Luke 16:19–31)

Jesus was good at reminding people about the eternal perspective. He said, "Whoever wants to be my disciple must deny themselves and take up their cross daily and follow me. For whoever wants to save their life will lose it, but whoever loses their life for me will save it. What good is it for someone to gain the whole world, and yet lose or forfeit their very self?" (Luke 9:23–25).

Is Jesus a killjoy? No, He wants us to be joyful, both in the short run and the long run. He knows that living for ourselves and pretending we're owners instead of stewards is bad for us. But when we "seek first his kingdom and his righteousness" (Matthew 6:33), we'll experience life the way God intends for us—a life lived to the full.

When we become stewards, we advance a different view of the world—one that aligns with the way things really are. This "alternative reality" means God cares about everything. The Great Commission—that we should make disciples of all nations—is often misunderstood to mean the only thing that matters is saving souls. There are several problems with this truncated view.

> When we become stewards, we advance a different view of the world—one that aligns with the way things really are.

First, to be a disciple means to be a Christ-follower—and that's a far cry from simply giving mental assent. Jesus expected some people to leave their occupations to follow Him around Israel. But all people who were His disciples were expected to make Him the center of their lives. Responding to an altar call may be the beginning of following Jesus, but it shouldn't be the end. James wrote that real faith will necessarily express itself in deeds. What deeds? Caring for widows and orphans, among other things (see James 1). The fundamentally Gnostic idea that God cares only about what we believe, not what we do is at odds with the gospel. "Show me your faith without deeds, and I will show you my faith by my deeds" (James 2:18).

Second, we can't save anyone; only God can do that. We invite people to follow Jesus, but we can't make it happen. We've tried. It just doesn't work. People have freedom to choose whether to surrender to God's will. In *The Brothers Karamazov* by Fyodor Dostoevsky (a favorite novel and deeply meaningful to us), one of the brothers, Ivan, rejects God because He's given humans freedom to rebel—ironically, the very thing Ivan is doing. Freedom is at the heart of the gospel. Jesus allowed the rich young ruler to walk away sad rather than coercing him into giving away all his wealth to follow Him.

Third, the Great Commission doesn't override other biblical imperatives, including the Cultural Commission. Nancy Pearcey and Chuck Colson wrote in the classic book *How Now Shall We Live?*,

> Evangelism and cultural renewal are both divinely ordained duties. God exercises his sovereignty in two ways: through *saving grace* and *common grace*. We are all familiar with saving grace; it is the means by which God's power calls people who are dead in their trespasses

and sins to new life in Christ. But few of us understand common grace, which is the means by which
God's power sustains creation, holding back the sin and
evil that result from the fall and that otherwise would
overwhelm His creation like a great flood. As agents of
God's common grace, we are called to help sustain and
renew his creation, to uphold the created institutions of
family and society, to pursue science and scholarship,
to create works of art and beauty, and to heal and help
those suffering from the results of the Fall.[12]

Advancing the kingdom of God includes inviting people to follow Jesus. But it also includes advancing justice for
the oppressed—even if they never became Christ-followers.
Justice and mercy aren't just God's "tools of the trade" in win-
ning souls—they're integral to the gospel. Try this thought
experiment: Would God want you to work to release girls
from forced prostitution even if you could know in advance
that they wouldn't become Christians? Of course! It's why
we don't just give to missionaries but also give to poverty
alleviation and poverty prevention ministries—and it's why
we invest in businesses run according to God's principles.
We should care about all of God's directives, not just the
Great Commission.

In case you need any more convincing, in Jesus's parable about the sheep and the goats (Matthew 25), note
what the sheep did that the goats didn't do: They provided
food and drink and shelter and clothing and medicine and
prison visitation. It's interesting that Jesus did not mention preaching and leading Bible studies. It's not that those

things aren't important (they are); rather, Jesus is suggesting here that salvation isn't *only* about preaching the Word but also living it out in all its manifestations.

We know people sometimes worry that prioritizing anything other than missions and evangelism leads to a "social gospel" that becomes a religion of good works alone—exactly what's happened to many mainline churches that now look more like social clubs. That's a danger, but a bigger danger is eviscerating Jesus's words to construct our own lopsided gospel. Jesus cares about salvation and poverty and forced labor and poverty and, and, and. . . . The kingdom is about saving souls *and* doing justice, loving mercy, and walking humbly with God (Micah 6:8).

There's another reason we steward our resources: "Where your treasure is, there your heart will be also" (Matthew 6:21). Our resource allocation reflects and shapes our hearts. Someone who spends all their time, money, and mental energy improving their golf score loves golf. The question is whether they love God more than golf. Only God can answer that question, but it's a question we should be asking ourselves. The choices we make with our resources shape our souls. That's why we wrestle with our spending—we want to present ourselves as living sacrifices, not conformed to worldly patterns but transformed by the gospel (Romans 12:1).

Stewardship is principally done to glorify God, not as a means of getting rich. Good stewardship of our resources *might* lead to more wealth—financially and socially—but it might *not*. Christians starve to death and go bankrupt and suffer just as non-Christians do. We know people who faithfully followed the Lord but had unmet temporal needs. They did well spiritually, but they still suffered loss. (See more on this in chapter 7 on the dangers of wealth.)

The last point we want to make about why we steward is this: It leads to human flourishing. We were created to be givers, investors, savers, and risk-takers. We weren't made to own what isn't ours to own. Just as we were made to serve instead of being served, we were made to use God's resources to love Him, others, His magnificent creation, and ourselves (all in proper proportion).

What We Steward

The question of what we steward is simple: everything. There's nothing subject to our influence or control that we don't steward: our money, time, body, reputation, family, friends, talent, skills, and so on. The key is not to *own* any of it in our hearts and to always recognize it's on loan from God and we could lose it at any time.

This doesn't mean we can't *enjoy* what the Lord has given us. The apostle Paul wrote to his protégé Timothy that God "richly provides us with everything for our enjoyment" (1 Timothy 6:17). There's a place for feasting, vacations, premium coffee, fancy restaurants, nice cars, and every good thing under the sun—but only under His lordship.

Dana:

I love adventure and experiences. Despite my sometimes-absurd frugality, when our family is on vacation, I open the purse strings to pay for experiences. When we were visiting the

Grand Canyon, I didn't bat an eye paying for the helicopter ride, nor did I think twice about paying for the kids and my thrill-seeking husband to do a twelve-story freefall into a net. (They all came back alive!) At first, I totally surprised Bill, who's used to my frugality, but now he gets it. Still, my penny-pinching tendencies come back into play when it comes to staying at nice hotels and eating at fancy restaurants. Bill and I sometimes have a tug of war over those things. I want to be cautious about living a luxurious lifestyle, which wouldn't be good for my soul. The question is one of stewardship and honoring the Lord, both in your times of feasting and times of "normal life."

Each of us must steward all we have to please the Lord, but that will mean different things for different people.

Greg Baumer: Seeing Money like God Does

Greg Baumer was on the fast track to riches. He scored big when he went to work for the premiere corporate consulting firm McKinsey, which then opened the door for him to attend Harvard Business School.

"My identity was defined by career success early on," Greg told us. He was already a committed Christian and a tither. He saw his parents quietly and consistently practice generosity, but Greg thought of giving as an obligatory checkbox for a "good" Christian—not as a radical means of reflecting God's character that has world-changing consequences. "Growing up, my church almost never talked about money. It never occurred to me that my faith and money intersected," Greg said.

During his graduate studies, Greg had an opportunity to take a Harvard Divinity School class on Christian financial stewardship, opening the door for him to interview two hundred Christian Harvard Business School alumni. "That was my Saul-to-Paul moment," he told us. He talked with a hedge fund manager earning $10 million a year who gave away everything he earned. Before spending anything above $2,500, he'd seek permission from an informal council of Christian brothers. "The guy wanted to buy a golf cart to drive around the neighborhood with his kids, but he wouldn't do it without getting permission from his accountability group." (They told him, "Dude, buy it!")

Greg interviewed another wealthy businessman who allowed a group of fellow Christians to set his annual salary because he didn't trust himself to handle money well. "The thing that struck me was how much joy he experienced from his massive generosity," Greg said. "It was super compelling. I hadn't seen the authentic depth of joy prior to that." Greg believes that Christians' tenacious hold on money is the biggest impediment to experiencing wholehearted life in Jesus for many people in the Western world.

Greg and his classmate, John Cortines, turned their research into a book—*God and Money*—which contends that God calls Christians to give abundantly and to lay aside their tendencies to become spenders or savers. Money management is important, but generosity is nearer to the heart of God. Greg's grateful he learned these lessons early in his career when he still had a negative net worth, because it equipped him to be generous once he started to earn serious money.

Money management is important, but
generosity is nearer to the heart of God.

"The question flipped from, *How much should I give?*
to *How much do I really need to keep?*" Greg said. Asking
the question this way reminds us that everything we have
belongs to God and can be stewarded for His purposes. For
Greg and his wife, Alison, this has meant setting a "finish
line"—capping their annual spending and saving and giving away the rest.

Writing a book about generosity doesn't mean Greg has
it all figured out. He still wrestles with how much to spend
and on what. Before Greg and Alison decided to build a
new home, Greg was in turmoil, grappling with whether
that was a luxury he shouldn't afford, even though they
could afford it. As He so often does, the Holy Spirit spoke
into Greg's life via a friend, giving Greg the conditional
liberty to build the house—providing it was used generously and for regular hospitality. "It was permission with a
caveat," Greg said.

He laments, "Money remains such a taboo topic in the
church. I suspect the Lord will say to many of us, 'Nice
job, you did a great job on lifting people out of poverty
and combating sex trafficking, but you committed the sin
of materialism every minute of your life and didn't even
realize it.'"

Greg and Alison have been fighting the church's reti-
cence to discuss money by starting a giving group in their

community, seeking to collectively make large gifts to non-profits and have a bigger impact. "We've found so much joy in expressing generosity with others," Greg said.

Coming together as a couple in their stewardship has required balancing Greg's love of spreadsheets and structured giving with Alison's love of spontaneity. To make it work for both of them, Alison has a budgeted "slush fund" that she can use for generosity at the spur of a moment.

"I'm convinced our lives should look markedly different than our peers because of Jesus, especially when it comes to money," Greg said. "Living this out so it's more than just head knowledge requires regularly wrestling with the Holy Spirit."

We're grateful that Greg wrestles with the Lord and wrote down what he's learned in a book about two of our favorite topics: God and money.

How We Steward

Greg's story demonstrates that stewarding is more art than science. The Lord could have given us a rule book on stewardship, but He didn't. He gives us broad guidelines in Scripture and leaves the specifics to us to discern. Those guidelines are that we should steward

1. with prayer;
2. in community; and
3. with careful planning.

First, we must steward with prayer. We each spend time in prayer listening for the Lord's voice. We know not everyone has had a sense of hearing God speak to them, but we have. Sometimes it's a strong thought that comes to mind out of nowhere. Other times, we hear the Lord in a sermon or a podcast or conversation. However it happens, it feels to us like we've heard Him inaudibly speak to our spirits in that "still small voice" (1 Kings 19:12 KJV).

Could we be wrong? Definitely. History is replete with people who think they've heard God tell them to fly airplanes into buildings or take drugs or any number of crazy things. That's why we need to be humble about what we think we've heard and measure it against Scripture and in community with fellow Christians.

We love the story of one of our friends who was blessed with huge wealth and is radically generous but was struggling with whether it would be morally acceptable to buy a Porsche. This friend could have afforded to buy a fleet of Porsches without making a dent in his wealth. The question was whether that would please the Lord. After prayer, he ordered the Porsche, but then he had second thoughts and canceled the order the next day. But he wrestled some more and felt he had the Lord's liberty to do it, so he called the dealership again and reordered the car. Then he felt conflicted again and canceled the order. Finally, he prayed through it again and felt the liberty to do so, but this time he called a different dealership to place the order, sparing himself the embarrassment! He drove it in joy for many years.

The point of the story is that our friend was seeking to please the Lord with everything, including his car choice. For another person, driving anything more than an old minivan would be out of bounds. There are no bright lines about what's allowable for each person. We need to listen carefully for that "still small voice" to discern what the Lord may want for us.

Second, we must steward in community. So often, the Lord directs us through His people, which is why Dennis and Eileen Bakke were willing to open their finances to their small group—such an amazing act of humility and accountability. We were made to live out our faith with others, and it's one prevalent means of hearing the Lord direct us. We make a habit of being in small groups with other Christ-followers, as we've both done for most of our adult lives. Proverbs says, "Plans fail for lack of counsel, but with many advisers they succeed" (Proverbs 15:22).

Author Andy Crouch goes as far as to tell people how much he earns, his net worth, and his giving. He insists that given the money isn't ours to begin with, it's only sensible to share our finances with fellow Christians. We've done it with some wise and godly friends, though we've not been as free sharing it as Andy. The point is that we need each other to help us think through the best way to steward the Lord's resources entrusted to our care.

Third, we must steward with careful planning. Good decisions are often made in advance. That's what the Chapmans did (in chapter 1), deciding to give away 50 percent of whatever they earned through the sale of their business well before the business even generated revenue. The apostle Paul instructed the Corinthian church to think ahead and then follow through: "Each of you should give what you have decided in your heart to give, not reluctantly or under compulsion, for God loves a cheerful giver" (2 Corinthians 9:7).

Planning is so important, so we want to flesh this out a bit more in the following.

The Joy of . . . Budgeting[13]

Not many people like to budget or keep track of their expenses. But we do. That makes us a bit . . . unusual. Still, we'd like to make the case for the increased joy that comes from following a budget.

Yes, joy. Giving is much more fun when you've already decided how much you'll give away. Donating to charities becomes a question of *where* to give rather than how much to give. There's no pain in thinking about how much money you're forgoing because you've already given it away in your heart. If at least 10 percent of your money is automatically designated to be given away, then deciding where to give feels like using free tickets at a carnival.

Second, saying no to emotional appeals for a charity that lies outside your planned giving is less heart-wrenching. Once you have given your planned amount, it's easier not to feel guilty about *not* giving. Your budget has been set, and you can feel more at peace about saying no. But if you don't have an agreed-on amount to give away, you may find yourself wrestling with every appeal.

> If you don't have an agreed-on amount to give away, you may find yourself wrestling with every appeal.

It's not true that we should always give more. It's possible to give away more money than the Lord wants—and we know people who have done just that and later regret it. All our money belongs to God, not just the portion we give away. The Lord has given us responsibilities to pay our bills, save for the future, care for our families, and so on. It may well be ungodly to give to charity what should go elsewhere. A careful, prayerful plan, well-executed, is pleasing to God.

Is it possible that the Lord might call us to change our plans and give more than we budgeted? Sure, He does that sometimes. But most of the time, a thoughtful plan bathed in prayer is how the Lord leads.

If you live within a budget for your lifestyle and your tithe, what about spontaneous generosity that falls in the gray area not typically thought of as charitable giving? If you're too planned, wouldn't that preclude on-the-spot generosity that flows from compassion or awareness of a new and important need? Nope—not if you plan for that too. We budget a specific percentage of our gross income (above our other planned giving) for spontaneous, non-tax-deductible giving. That way, we can pay for a friend's meal or anything else that wouldn't usually be considered "charity" where there isn't a true need. This can still be an expression of generosity. Here again, giving becomes more fun when it's part of a responsible plan.

We also build in flexibility with our regular planned tithe, setting aside money for the inevitable appeals that we can't predict but want to respond to (short-term mission trips, for example). If it doesn't get used during the year, it gets added to one of our regular charities. Hence, we build flexibility into our planned and unplanned giving. We do the same for our saving and investing, dedicating different percentages to different risk/reward profiles, all through a kingdom perspective.

It's true that budgeting still means saying no to spending outside the budget, and that's never easy. But that's what stewardship is all about—saying no to some things so we can say yes to other things.

Budgeting also leads to peace in other areas of our lives. For instance, budgeting for "unexpected" auto expenses just makes good sense, and it can help reduce stress when our car breaks down—because it's already in the budget. It also injects reality into our budgeting and makes us realize how little truly discretionary income we really have.

There's another cost of budgeting: keeping track of your expenses. Budgets can lie, but an accurate record of actual expenses doesn't. It's easy to draft a hopelessly unrealistic budget, as we did ourselves the first year of our marriage. We kept thinking we could live on less than we could. But a budget based on last year's actual expenses, adjusted for the cost of living, is far more likely to be a *real* budget. Plus, it helps us confront those uncomfortable truths—like knowing how much we really spent at Starbucks. Once we know the truth, we can better make needed adjustments. Not keeping track of expenses may be a way of shielding us from what we'd rather not know.

It's a hassle to keep track of expenses, but there are so many useful tools to make tracking expenses easier. Many software programs can help us assign categories to expenses downloaded from a bank or credit card account. Spending a couple of hours each month keeping track of expenses is worth the freedom of living in reality.

For the ambitious, categorizing your giving (church, evangelism, discipleship, poverty, cultural renewal, etc.) can help you decide how much to give to specific areas. We tend to give more money to areas that receive less of our time (since giving of our time is another form of stewardship). There's no magic formula, but examining your giving and planning is another metric to help you lean into the joy of intentional living.

Following a budget can help us experience more joy in serving God by what we give, spend, save, and invest. It's not easy, but the effort pays dividends in decreased stress and increased joy. And we are promised that our planned and steady giving will never be in vain.

Patrick Fisher: Business as Ministry

"We are so skewed in our thinking about capital. Christians clip the wings of so many people who have great business talents, asking them just to make money only so they can give it to the church," said Patrick Fisher, a successful asset manager and founder of Creation Investments Capital Management, a private equity firm. Patrick's calling is to profitably use investment capital to help low-income people get access to loans so they can also make money. His business isn't a machine generating cash only to make

tax-deductible donations to ministries; rather, it's a ministry in its own right, empowering people to flourish using
investment capital for scale and impact.

Patrick has an MBA from the Kellogg School of Management at Northwestern University—one of the best business schools in the country. After excelling at JPMorgan
Chase, Patrick believed the Lord was calling him to take
a one-year sabbatical to work at his church. "I needed to
put to death the need for status, and working at my church
helped me do that. God also put to death a lot of my desires
to amass huge wealth. Even so, the Lord has brought me
enormous financial success, but now it doesn't control me,"
Patrick said. "It's under the lordship of Christ."

Patrick never returned to JPMorgan—but not because
he kept working at the church, as you might expect. Patrick
was made for business, and he felt the Lord calling him to
return to the business world, but this time by starting his
own private equity firm with an explicit mission to provide
financial services to the world's poor who are overlooked,
neglected, and excluded by traditional banks. He named it
Creation because Patrick believes that wealth is created, not
exchanged, with market forces being God's main framework of providing for our financial needs.

Creation is guided by one goal: "to reduce poverty
and its ill effects in the developing world by increasing
access to capital and other financial services to those at
the bottom of the economic pyramid." Today, Creation
has $2.2 billion in assets under management with over
$15 billion in loans outstanding, mostly to low-income

women in the developing world who would otherwise be deemed not creditworthy by established banks. Creation has 44 million customers and 71,000 employees, and Creation's investors have outperformed market returns—demonstrating that serving the poor and market returns are not mutually exclusive.

Some people believe that a business focused on serving the Lord must be explicitly proclaiming the gospel. Patrick disagrees. "We don't serve low-income people in the developing world because they're Christians, but because we are," Patrick said. "My business is all about *declaring* the gospel, not *proclaiming* it. We give a cup of cold water to the thirsty because we care about them. Our core work empowers people to thrive."

The lack of access to capital is a clear contributor to poverty and accentuates the wealth gap. Patrick points to the redlining that deprived African Americans access to home mortgages as an injustice that has perpetuated the legacy of discrimination. "Loans to the poor can have a massive impact, propelling wealth creation, greater access to nutrition, health, and education—which are all components of human flourishing."

Patrick believes that bad thinking about basic economics hurts people. He's seen how well-intentioned charities have undermined human dignity instead of enhancing it. "Larger, systemic charity tends to lead to bureaucracy and ultimately an exploitive power grab of the very group you're trying to serve—and a dependency that is bad for the human soul," he said.

In contrast, a biblical view of economics recognizes the Creation Mandate—God's command to flourish and have dominion—that leads to the multiplication of resources and can lift people out of poverty to fulfill their God-given potential via dignifying work.

Patrick believes that market forces, when properly structured, "empower people, giving them choice and agency," thereby making people into customers instead of recipients of endless charity. "Jobs, opportunities, and wealth are created when we follow God's game plan for creation. Working with His design for the world leads to vibrancy." And Patrick believes that market forces and business play a central role in human well-being.

Patrick hasn't let his tremendous business success cloud his vision. He drives an old car, and he and his family live in a house far below their means in a diverse urban neighborhood of Chicago. He sees all his capital—both charitable and noncharitable—as belonging to the Lord. Patrick said, "My job is to follow God in whatever He calls me to do. Period. The Lord wants me to be faithful in the little things. If He decides to 'move the decimals,' great; if not, no problem. Stewardship is the key."

Kate's, Greg's, and Patrick's stories of faithful stewardship illustrate that everything belongs to God, and we will be called to give an account of how we use our money. The kingdom of God is the most important thing, and we dare not neglect the Lord's command to do justice and be merciful even as we seek to persuade others to follow Christ.

Salvation is not all that matters to God. We steward our resources according to God's principles not as a means of getting wealthy but of being faithful. Inherent in God's economy is responsible risk-taking, which helps us to flourish. We steward our resources with prayer, in community with fellow Christ-followers, and with forethought.

God Loves Multiplication (and Profit)

Profit is like oxygen, food, water, and blood for the body; they are not the point of life, but without them, there is no life.

—Jim Collins and Jerry Porras, *Built to Last*

John and Sarah Bolin: Leveraging Profit for Evangelism

"People just kept telling us we shouldn't be making money on the gospel," John Bolin told us. "And we listened to them—until we decided to listen to the Lord instead."

In 1997, youth ministers John and Sarah Bolin wrote *The Thorn*, a powerful and moving stage show about the life of Christ featuring music, drama, aerial acts, dance, and big visual effects. Their first audience was two hundred high school kids, and it was an instant success. The show was communicating the beauty of the gospel in a dramatic and creative fashion.

One audience member said, "My life was changed at *The Thorn*. I couldn't stop crying—a gut-wrenching sobbing. As I watched the performance, I thought that if He did that for me then the least I could do is give Him my life, my heart, and my soul. I immediately entered a very deep and personal relationship with my Jesus. Thank you, God!" The Bolins have many similar testimonials from theatergoers.

For twenty-six years, the play traveled around the country, supported by ticket sales and donations—including donations from the Bolins' own bank account. John said, "The play wasn't sustainable financially. It was barely scraping by, propped up by the books I was writing. It was a labor of love. The first year we took the show on the road, we lost a half-million dollars. But we wanted people to see it."

The shows were usually sold out—a hit show with great reviews that's not making money.

"John didn't want to raise the ticket prices to make it work financially," Sarah told us. "I was trying to convince him, but he insisted that he wanted to keep the price low so people could afford to see it." Well-motivated? Yes. But there was a problem.

"I finally had to drop out of helping with the production," John said. "I needed to make money to pay our bills, so I turned to full-time writing and Sarah ran the show alone. I came to resent *The Thorn* because of how it was holding us back financially. And Sarah felt like the show's quality was suffering without my help."

John said, "Then, we had a conversation with friends who challenged us to rethink our decision to be a nonprofit. They told us that there's nothing wrong with making a profit—and by becoming a for-profit production, we could free up charitable dollars for nonprofits that had to rely on donations. That changed everything. In our first year as a for-profit, we've expanded the audience sevenfold."

The Bolins stopped holding their performances in church venues and moved to public theaters. Sarah, who likes to mill around the foyer incognito before and after shows, immediately saw the audience change. "Now people come who would never darken the door of a church. They like what they see. It's showing them the gospel, many for the first time, in a format that's more understandable to them."

What began as a homemade play with volunteers has become a large, professional show with performers who receive market wages. The quality of the production is rising dramatically as more money flows in from the higher ticket prices and larger audiences. More than 1.5 million people have seen *The Thorn* on stage, and about 100,000 people have made decisions to follow the Lord after seeing it. Today, there's even a film version of the show that has been seen by 85,000 people.

John said, "Now I see there's no limit to where we could take *The Thorn*. I no longer see profit as a negative thing but as a God thing—if we keep our hearts clean."

Profit Built into the Creation Mandate

In the Genesis account of creation, God commands Adam and Eve to "be fruitful and increase in number; fill the earth and subdue it. Rule over the fish in the sea and the birds in the sky and over every living creature that moves on the ground" (Genesis 1:28). This means more than just having babies. Implicit in the command is the notion of multiplication of people *and* resources. In other words, use the gifts God's given you to create something useful, just as the Bolins are doing.

Investopedia defines profit as "the financial benefit realized when revenue generated from a business activity exceeds the expenses, costs, and taxes involved in sustaining the activity in question."[14] If it costs you one dollar to run a business so you can earn one dollar, it wouldn't make financial sense to do it. Outputs need to exceed inputs to "be fruitful and increase." That's profit.

We know many believers are uncomfortable with the idea that profit is part of God's plan. It's understandable, given how often profit is castigated in academic and popular media. Many people assume that to earn profit inherently means to take advantage of someone else. The ideal, some argue, is to charge no more than something costs to produce plus a very small margin for the business to keep its lights on.

We know many believers are
uncomfortable with the idea that
profit is part of God's plan.

Dana:

I was enamored with this thinking during my early adult years. I was a proud Christian socialist, interned at a socialist think tank, and even dated a Communist during college. I thought that business and profit were inherently wrong. When I spent a year living in a socialist country—taking a four-hour round trip just to make a phone call back to the United States and generally being astounded at the endemic inefficiencies—I came to recognize the superiority of market economies.

Consider a world in which businesses just barely scrape by. How could new inventions ever come about without the possibility of profit? How would a growing population be sustained? How would we get groundbreaking medical advancements that save millions of lives?

Profit isn't optional for a flourishing society; it's absolutely necessary. Profit empowers us to "subdue" the earth and "rule over" every living creature. It's why few of us in the West know many mothers who have died in childbirth—something commonplace in poor countries and in our own history. It's why we can go on vacations or have automobiles or go camping in dry tents. There is no evidence that God wanted us to lead a subsistence life—which is a life almost wholly devoid of profit. To the contrary, the biblical ideal is prospering cities and farms with feast times and bountiful harvests. None of this can happen without profit.

Of course, exploitation—which is a form of excessive profit that takes advantage of other people—is unbiblical. That's one reason the West has antitrust laws to prevent businesses from colluding to fix prices at the expense of consumers. But working hard, taking risks, innovating, and reaping a bountiful financial harvest is a blessing from God that blesses far more people than just the entrepreneur. That entrepreneur can then turn and be a blessing to others, provide employment to people who need jobs, and develop new products that bring flourishing to an entire society.

Both inside and outside the church, profit is often associated with greed and benefiting from others' misfortune or needs. In contrast, nonprofits are often esteemed as more trustworthy. Consider all the nonprofits we value: hospitals, schools, churches, homeless shelters, prison ministries, youth organizations, and the like. We often think of nonprofits as doing things solely in the interest of the targeted audience.

Like most things, there's often some truth to this. Nonprofit employees usually earn less money than their peers in for-profit businesses. Nonprofits count on the generosity of donors to survive. And for-profit businesses do sometimes take advantage of customers. But the converse is also true: Sometimes nonprofit organizations waste other people's money, are woefully inefficient, and thrive on other people's problems. The greater the need, the easier time the nonprofit has raising money. Frequently, businesses do a better job addressing human needs, are more efficient and cost-effective, and are more responsive to customers. And businesses that fail their customers will usually go out of business when a more customer-friendly competitor emerges, whereas ineffective nonprofits can go on and on.

More fundamentally, there's an underlying assumption that when revenues exceed costs, something is crooked.

This notion comes from Karl Marx, who argued capitalism is predicated on the financial exploitation of the majority by a minority. That's not a biblical idea. "Fruitfulness" entails harvesting more than was planted. Bountiful harvests, increasing flocks, and hard work leading to wealth are lauded in Scripture. Proverbs 10:4 says, "Lazy hands make for poverty, but diligent hands bring wealth."

Jesus's parable of the talents lauds the servant who multiplied his master's initial capital: "Well done, good and faithful servant! You have been faithful with a few things; I will put you in charge of many things. Come and share your master's happiness!" (Matthew 25:21). The master praised his servant for making a huge profit. And the servant who returned his master's initial capital without a profit was condemned: "You wicked, lazy servant! So you knew that I harvest where I have not sown and gather where I have not scattered seed? Well then, you should have put my money on deposit with the bankers, so that when I returned I would have received it back with interest" (Matthew 25:26–27). Jesus portrayed the master as using harsh language to underscore the importance God places on multiplying His resources.

When interpreting Scripture, it can be dangerous to argue from what the text *doesn't* say, so we want to tread carefully here. But we suspect that even if the most successful servant had *lost* his master's wealth through a bold but unsuccessful business endeavor, the master still would have been pleased with the effort. The parable was meant to demonstrate that God loves multiplication, not that He punishes well-intentioned failures. The servant who buried the talent was punished because he didn't even try to earn a profit. Effort and intention are what matter to God.

It's important to note that profit isn't an unqualified good; it's good only when it's been properly earned and used well. Exploitation and greed are contrary to God's ways: "The greedy bring ruin to their households, but the one who hates bribes will live" (Proverbs 15:27). We know this intuitively. In the wake of a Florida hurricane, when the water filtration system is offline, it would be wrong for someone to charge $15 for a bottle of water that costs just pennies to produce. But if the law forbade making *any* profit, few people would ship water to the region. Profit within ethical bounds is good and even necessary to bring needed services to customers.

There was a joke about the communist Soviet Union that captures an essential truth: eggs were only a dime a dozen (thanks to government price controls) . . . but there were no eggs! Without profit, people suffer—especially the poor and those without political power. Profit is integral to God's design for the world. We eschew it at our peril.

What's Profit For?

Jim Collins and Jerry Porras wrote that "profit is like oxygen, food, water, and blood for the body; they are not the point of life, but without them, there is no life."[15] To put it simply, then, profit generates the margin that enables our world to function, funding families, communities, governments, and nonprofits. It's not an end in itself but rather a means to an end—namely, human flourishing.

God loves profit because He loves life. Profit increases, enriches, and beautifies life. Profit is an essential tool in God's plan of creation, and He loves both addition and multiplication.

> Profit is an essential tool in God's plan of creation, and He loves both addition and multiplication.

Think about just a few of the many blessings God bestows on us through the multiplication of His resources: antibiotics, anesthesia, theaters, stadiums, sailboats (Bill thinks this is one of God's best earthly gifts!), coffee, shoes, New York strip steak—this list could be infinitely longer, but you get the idea. Prosperity showers humanity with so many good gifts that beautify and enrich our lives. Think we're overstating things? Then just consider the standard living conditions of societies that inhibit wealth creation and deplore profits. They are not nice places to live.

Bill:

I lived in what was then West Berlin, Germany, after graduating from college. I lived one block from the infamous Berlin Wall that separated West (free) and East (Communist) Berlin. The Wall was meant to keep East Berliners from escaping to the West. At least one hundred and forty East Germans were killed trying to cross to the West, including five people during the time I lived close to Checkpoint Charlie. My neighborhood was heinously interrupted by the Wall, which was really two walls separated by a hundred yards called "the death strip" with guard towers, snipers, mines, and barbed wire.

For a $3 visa and $12 exchanged into low-value East German Marks, a US citizen could cross through the checkpoints and spend the day in the Communist East—something I did twice. East Berlin was praised as the "showcase of Communism," but I soon realized that if this was the best Communism had to offer, it wasn't worth much. Drab, Soviet-style buildings and long lines of unsmiling citizens waiting for tasteless soft drinks and bland bratwurst painted the picture of life in a totalitarian state. The empty store shelves were testament to the fact that profit was forbidden. Without an incentive to produce, the famous German work ethic was expunged. When the Wall finally came down in 1989, it took years for industriousness to be restored in the East.

In June 1987, I heard that President Ronald Reagan was coming to Berlin to give a speech at the Brandenburg Gate. I called the US embassy and received a ticket to attend. I stood near the front and clapped along with the thousands of people in the crowd as the president spoke these now historic words:

> *General Secretary Gorbachev, if you seek peace, if you seek prosperity for the Soviet Union and Eastern Europe, if you seek liberalization: Come here to this gate! Mr. Gorbachev, open this gate! Mr. Gorbachev, tear down this wall![16]*

Two-and-a-half years later, the Wall was torn down—to the shock of the whole world. East Germany slowly became prosperous. Ten years later, I returned to my old neighborhood, no longer fractured by the Wall. In fact, where the Wall had stood was almost imperceptible as it had become a greenway with maturing trees and green grass. Store shelves were well stocked, and the infamous Stasi (secret police) were gone. With the advent of liberty came the freedom for businesses to profit, and with profit, life returned to the once-drab neighborhood.

Profit is one way that God designed the world to be life-giving. Profit, procured and employed in God's way, leads to abundance and life.

Jon Porter: A Calling to Serve in Business

"I wanted to move to Haiti to work in an orphanage, but the Lord said to me, 'No, I want you to go into business,'" said Jon Porter—the opposite of the kind of calling we usually hear spoken from a missionary at a Sunday night service.

As a USC business major, Jon planned to go into business—until he took a trip to Haiti that in his words "really messed me up. Haiti is just ninety minutes from Miami, and the wealth disparity just blew my mind." Jon went back to Haiti two more times during college, and that reoriented his career path to working in a Haitian orphanage. "I saw kids starving by the side of the road, and I thought, *What else can I do with my life other than fight for the poor and the oppressed?*"

For many people, their great fear is not getting a decent job. Jon's greatest fear was living an insignificant life. "For me, having a great career and making lots of money seemed like an easy way to be lulled into insignificance. But moving to Haiti to work with orphans? That felt significant."

In his senior year, Jon decided to apply for an internship with a prominent consulting firm "just in case" he couldn't go to Haiti. It was an extremely competitive internship—just two openings for twenty applicants, and everyone was very qualified.

Jon told us, "I was sitting in the parking garage in downtown LA at 7 a.m., ahead of a grueling eight-hour round of interviews, asking myself, 'Why am I here? I don't want this internship. I want to go serve the poor.' And that's when I had my first radical encounter with God. In a flash, God's presence entered the vehicle. I could almost physically feel God resting on me. I stopped praying and just started weeping—overwhelmed at the presence of God. Then, His presence left just as fast as it came, taking with it every ounce of fear and intimidation about the interviews."

"I asked myself, 'Why did that just happen? Why here and why now?' I didn't know, but I went into the interviews and knocked it out of the park. I left at the end of the day knowing I'd get the offer. And a week later, I did. I knew I was supposed to go into business instead of moving to Haiti," Jon said.

"For me, going to Haiti required less faith than going into business. How was I going to avoid a life of insignificance in business?" Jon asked himself. Jon succeeded in the internship, helping Fortune 50 CEOs get better compensation—"literally as far as I could get from rescuing kids in Haiti."

The firm offered him a job upon graduation.

Jon was a good student, and he graduated early—six months before his job was scheduled to begin. "I had time to kill, and I found a consulting firm in Rwanda, combining my love of business with my love for the poor. Eventually, I decided that this was what God had up His sleeve all along," Jon said. Instead of returning to the United States to claim his $80,000-a-year job, he stayed in Rwanda and worked for $24,000 a year.

After a few years, he applied for a 100,000-euro grant from the Dutch embassy in Rwanda to launch a dairy processing enterprise. To his surprise, he won. He bought the equipment of a failed yogurt processor and launched Masaka Farms in 2015. Within a year, Masaka was on a steady growth trajectory. "Then the Lord threw me another curveball: He encouraged me to hire a deaf woman whose daughter was in a coma. Sometimes you just know that God has spoken to you," he said.

As crazy as it seemed, Jon did it. But then he realized he needed to hire more deaf people so they could communicate with one another in sign language. Now a majority of Masaka Farms employees are deaf—"and they're amazing to work with," Jon said. "They're hard workers and committed to the company that gave them a chance to rise above the stigma placed on them. It turns out, hiring the deaf was a fantastic business decision."

Today, Masaka Farms is successful and growing and recently became Rwanda's top-selling brand of yogurt. It's generating profits for its investors and providing meaningful and dignified jobs for people who are otherwise unemployable. Its employees can afford food on the table, a safe dwelling, and education and health care for their kids. Plus, it provides protein to Rwanda's population, which is critical to prevent childhood malnutrition.

It does all of this without relying on charitable contributions, unlike a nonprofit.

Jon is back in California but continues to serve as the chairman of the company's board, cheerleading for it from half a world away: "My calling remains the same: To do business in partnership with Him, living life without a sacred/secular divide."

Imagine if Jon had not listened to the Lord's call to go into business and Masaka Farms had never existed! God doesn't just call missionaries; He calls businesspeople too—calling them to produce profits that change the world, one job at a time. Through profitable businesses, jobs are sustainable, and the poor are no longer desperate for handouts. They can now be generous to others and help the less fortunate with hand-ups, to their joy and dignity.

There is an old parable about a person who sees a baby drowning as it floats downriver. The person jumps in to rescue the baby, but then more babies keep coming. More people are diving in to save the babies, except for one person who is running away from the rescue effort. "Where are you going?" shout the rescuers to the person running away. The person yells back, "I'm going upstream to stop someone from throwing babies in the water!"

Jon was called to go upstream to prevent poverty in the first place.

Business as Ministry

Jon's story paints in primary colors the truth that for-profit business blesses the world. Many seemingly intractable problems are best addressed through business, not traditional ministries and nonprofits. Sadly, Christians too often overestimate the role of nonprofit "ministries" and underestimate the role of for-profit businesses in advancing the kingdom of God. Businesspeople often get this message subtly or directly from the pulpit, making them feel like second-class Christians to the first-class Christians who are in "full-time ministry"—missionaries, pastors, and evangelists.

Every Christ-follower should be in full-time ministry, properly understood as doing all our work to glorify the Lord and advance His kingdom. The Westminster Shorter Catechism aptly identifies the chief end of humanity: "To glorify God and enjoy Him forever." We should never stop glorifying God, whether we're mopping floors, coding, selling insurance, or singing hymns. Our goal should be consistent with Paul's admonition, "So whether you eat or drink or whatever you do, do it all for the glory of God" (1 Corinthians 10:31).

This excludes nothing—except activities specifically proscribed by Scripture, like prostitution. There's just no way to be a prostitute to God's glory! Thankfully, there are few productive activities outside God's expansive view of creation. As the early twentieth-century theologian and Dutch prime minister Abraham Kuyper famously said, "There is not a square inch in the whole domain of our human existence over which Christ, who is Sovereign over all, does not cry: 'Mine!"[17]

The Lord has a plan for business just as much as He does for missions; they're equally important to Him. We know this statement may be jarring to many Christians steeped in the pietistic idea that evangelism and the Great Commission trump every other activity. But our call isn't just to "save souls." It's not we who save, anyway, but God; all we can do is invite people. Jesus's brother James said it best: "If one of you says to [someone in need], 'Go in peace; keep warm and well fed,' but does nothing about their physical needs, what good is it?" (James 2:16).

> The Lord has a plan for business just as much as He does for missions; they're equally important to Him.

Or, as the African proverb says, "Empty stomachs make for blocked ears."

The point is clear: God cares about every human need, not just explicitly spiritual needs.

Jon Porter is doing God's business when he provides meaningful and remunerative jobs in Rwanda. He's advancing God's kingdom every bit as much as the pastor preaching a sermon—and more so if Jon's motivations are pure and the pastor's are self-aggrandizing.

Businesses live in the real world of cold, hard facts—supply chains and delivery deadlines and product quality and customer satisfaction and stiff competition. This stark reality can be hard and cruel; businesses go bankrupt, people lose their jobs, and investors lose their money. But there's also something life-giving about what some see as the hard-edged business world: Competition drives businesses to satisfy customers' needs. If one business fails to meet customer expectations, another enterprising business will soon overtake it.

That's the market at work. In contrast, government agencies have little incentive to improve their performance. There's a reason we dread our trips to the Department of Motor Vehicles. The employees are usually rude, the wait times are long, and the instructions are often indecipherable. But what choice do we have? None. And that's the problem.

A competitive marketplace does a better job providing for many human needs—unless government regulations or corruption prevent competition. Well-intentioned measures to create "fairness" can lessen competition and create unnatural monopolies immune to customer dissatisfaction. Crime and corruption can also prevent businesses from effectively and efficiently addressing customer needs. Although there is a place for some limited regulations—for instance, to protect the environment even if dumping toxic waste in the river is cheaper and more efficient in the short term—they must be as light as possible to permit businesses to compete and create a thriving marketplace. Of course, there are human needs that business can't address, and that is where nonprofit organizations and governments are essential.

Business as an Agent of Change

Marketplaces can be powerful change agents. Contrast the role of businesses in market economies with those in state-controlled economies. Good luck naming one export from the former Soviet Union besides vodka! There was a reason the Communist bloc had an active commercial espionage program—real-world problem-solving emanated from the West's market economies, not the Eastern state-run businesses.

Bill:

> *When I lived in West Berlin, I was a missionary to Turkish guest workers. After World War II, there were too few German men left to rebuild their destroyed country, and Turks were invited in to fill the gaps. The Turks retained their Turkish citizenship and were slow to take on German language and habits. Although I speak German, I learned Turkish from my Turkish friends. One day, I was visiting some Turkish friends who owned a barber shop, and they were happily chatting with me when a German customer came in. No one was in the barber's chair, and the German clearly became frustrated and agitated as my friends continued to chat with me. I was uncomfortably watching the clash of cultures, foreseeing what would happen next: The German customer walked out in a huff. The Turks looked at one another in surprise and said, "What's wrong with him?" The problem was that the German had a Western approach to time, and the Turks had a Middle Eastern approach to time.*

This question of time has an enormous impact on the wealth of a nation. Wealthy countries prioritize time, and poor countries rarely do. To climb the wealth ladder, it's necessary for poor countries to approach time more like the West. It's true that there are some social benefits to a more relaxed approach to time, but it's never better for economic growth. This doesn't mean that nations should adopt every aspect of the West's highly individualist and materialistic worldview—certainly not! Still, a Western approach to timeliness can help lift many people out of poverty.

Churches are powerful change agents in many ways, but not necessarily in the realm of time management. What could a nonprofit organization do to change a poor nation's approach to time? Classes or lectures aren't likely to be effective. In contrast, business holds enormous potential to act as a powerful lever. Don Larson's cashew company in Mozambique (see chapter 2) pays a small bonus to every worker every day they show up on time. He could just as easily penalize workers who are late, but he prefers to use the carrot over the stick. Regardless, the crucible of profit-making is going to prosper the companies whose workers pay more attention to time because factory lines won't sit idle due to absent workers. This is but one concrete example of how businesses can powerfully alter culture and bring prosperity and its many attendant benefits to a people.

Lacking a profit motive often limits the effectiveness of nonprofits. We've noted the inefficiencies of many non-profit ministries: too many meetings, too little action. Without a competitive incentive produced by profits, ministries that raise money from philanthropists can persist years after they've ceased to be effective. Nonprofits are often bad at measuring impact, measuring outputs instead of outcomes (e.g., numbers of people trained as opposed to training retained and applied), or focusing on emotional anecdotes.

About twenty years ago, our church encouraged its youth to collect money to contribute to a nonprofit providing mosquito nets to people in Africa to prevent malaria. It was well-meaning and a good family opportunity for tangible service, or so we thought. We educated our kids about malaria and the attendant death and poverty that it creates, plus how a simple net over a bed could prevent this terrible disease. However, we didn't realize the nonprofit was purchasing the nets from a global supplier, not from the local suppliers to those African markets. Consequently, people were protected from malaria for a time, but the local suppliers of nets couldn't compete with free, and they eventually went out of business. Did the global nonprofit stay in for the long run to provide free nets? No, they moved on. Over time, more people were exposed to malaria and fewer local workers had jobs.

This phenomenon has been documented elsewhere. We suspect much of the foreign aid money poured into Haiti has had a similar result. Local business can't compete with free, and the normal reactions of using personal agency to build long-term and locally appropriate solutions to the problem are squelched. This is not to say that immediate relief in a disaster is not a moral good, but when relief doesn't move on to sustainable development and growth interventions, helping ends up hurting.

What does this mean for our generosity? First, we encourage you to not let the *perfect* be the enemy of the *good*. In our investing and giving, we cannot foresee all unintended consequences prior to action. However, we can set up systems and habits that move us toward becoming more educated and evidence-based donors and investors. Use groups like Charity Navigator and MinistryWatch in your due diligence. Use systems and habits for your investing as well. Spending a bit more time, money, and prayer could help you do more good and less harm. Even though our emotions are important in discerning our passions and encouraging us when we are tempted to quit or fall into despair, we shouldn't let emotions be the final arbiter of those with whom we partner to implement solutions to the problems we are called to solve. (We provide educational resources in appendix B for honing the craft of giving and investing for kingdom impact.)

The Power of Business

There's another reason for-profit businesses sometimes have a larger impact than nonprofits: sheer size. The $557 billion in annual charitable giving in the United States in 2023[18] is dwarfed by the $67 trillion in total US household investable assets[19] (includes listed company holdings, cash holdings, and debt-free residential property holdings). That means charitable giving represents eight-tenths of one percent of investable assets.

Annual Charitable Giving vs. Total Liquid Investable Assets in the USA (2023)

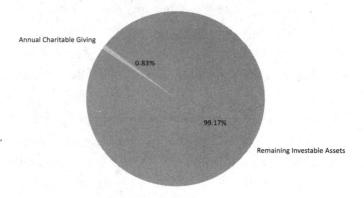

Consider how much time Christians spend thinking about that very small slice of charitable giving and how little we focus on the rest of the pie! For all the good nonprofits do—and we're big fans and supporters of many of them—they often lack the scale to do big things. For that, business is often far more effective.

Consider your own financial situation, comparing your annual charitable giving relative to your investable net worth (bank accounts, retirement accounts). You probably have more money available for investments than you give to charity. When you put money in a bank account, the bank deploys a significant portion in equity or debt investments in businesses. When you buy shares of a mutual fund, your money is invested in businesses. That's how you can expect to get back more money than you put in—businesses turning a profit, multiplying your resources. That process makes the pie larger, and we believe God intends for a growing pie to be distributed to both nonprofits and businesses in such a way that profit blesses people and planet.

That means God's people are sitting on a gold mine, though most of us are unaware of it. We hold fundraisers, contribute to food banks, participate in charity walk-a-thons, and host bake sales to raise money for charities that scrape by on our extra pennies—all good things. But we control vastly more money in our bank accounts, IRAs, 401(k)s, and our stock brokerages without contemplating what impact our investments are having or could have on the very things we're trying to address through charity. Yet the trillions of dollars under the control of Christians and the multiplying impact they have on the world are virtually ignored.

Our point isn't that business is necessarily better than nonprofits at contributing to human flourishing. But we are saying that we in the West place too much hope in nonprofits or government interventions and almost completely ignore the role God intended business to play.

Greg and Marybeth Lernihan: Multiplying Wealth for "the Least of These"

Legacy matters.

Greg Lernihan's Irish immigrant father often said, "Money is a nuisance." Greg's dad left his family's farm in Ireland at an early age so his parents would have one less mouth to feed.

Like many immigrants today, his journey to America led to starting a small business to survive. Greg told us his dad "observed many of the problems that people afflicted with wealth experience, and he wanted no part of that."

Greg's father never aspired to have wealth, nor did Greg. Greg believes that wealth is a matter of perspective. "My dad would say that we were wealthy—we had food, shelter, and we were able to go to school." That sense of gratitude and contentment runs deep in Greg, thanks to his father's modeling. His dad worked hard and tithed of his money and his time, providing Greg a solid example of faithful stewardship.

Greg was a high school senior and a basketball player when he took sophomore cheerleader Marybeth out for pizza on their first date on November 13, 1976. Today, the couple has been together for forty-seven years. After forty years of marriage, Greg and Marybeth are still sweethearts who love each other deeply—but they're in a far different place today than when they began their marriage.

When Greg and his business partner sold a controlling interest in their business in 2012, the Lernihans' bank account reached a level they had never dreamed about. Greg and Marybeth had mixed emotions. Greg said, "We didn't go to dinner or buy a new car. We ignored our wealth."

Marybeth chimed in, "Everything in our hearts warned us about the dangers of wealth. We were most concerned about the negative impact it could have on our children. Initially, it felt like a burden."

Early in the life of their company, Greg and his cofounder had voluntarily shared equity with key colleagues. When a portion of the company was sold twelve years later, those with ownership were huge beneficiaries—far beyond what anyone had dreamed. "Colleagues received varying amounts, and many received life-changing money," Greg said. "I loved telling the recipients what they would be getting. Some people cried, others jumped up from their chair, and most didn't believe it and thought we were joking. It changed so many lives."

One employee who had seven children surprised his wife in the middle of the night. While she was caring for their youngest baby, he came in and sat next to her—with a bottle of wine and two glasses—and said, "We don't have to worry anymore about paying for the kids' college!"

The Lord had been preparing the Lernihans for their wealth event. Greg had gone on a mission trip to Haiti a few months before the partial sale of the company. What he encountered on that trip changed him forever. He felt the gentle nudge of the Holy Spirit prompting him to leave the company he cofounded and repurpose his life toward one of significance.

"Upon leaving day-to-day operations, I thought I was going into the nonprofit world, but quickly learned that there are not enough charitable dollars to solve our global social problems. I was wired for the for-profit world and began exploring impact investing," Greg said.

That launched Greg and Marybeth in another direction: donating a portion of their wealth to a donor-advised fund for philanthropic purposes and investing in for-profit companies around the world that are led by Christians and provide jobs for the marginalized. Greg works with entrepreneurs and fund managers to seek triple-bottom-line returns on their investable dollars—spiritual, social, and financial returns.

Some of the Lernihans' family members have become involved in the stewarding of their resources. One of their sons oversees their faith-driven investing, their daughter-in-law leads their international grant-making, and their daughter serves as chair of their board. Greg and Marybeth slowly began to see their wealth in a different light. "Wealth in our eyes shifted from being a burden to becoming more of a responsibility," Marybeth said. Watching their adult children become active in the stewarding of wealth was a surprise and an immense joy.

Even amid their generosity, Greg and Marybeth were struggling spiritually and sought the Holy Spirit's input on whether God owned all their wealth. "That just seemed so crazy!" Greg said. "That's when I wrote this in my journal: 'Lord, help me to get comfortable giving all of the money away.'" That prayer slowly worked through Greg and Marybeth's spirits over a period of years, helping them to fully open their hands to the Lord.

They were able to spiritually release their money and decided to give most of their wealth away during their lifetime. Their financial advisors thought they had lost their minds! But that step liberated the Lernihans from initially viewing their wealth as a burden, then as a responsibility, to finally seeing it as a blessing. "We have grown spiritually. We see God interwoven in the whole journey. We feel called to steward His money with the Holy Spirit's guidance, and it's been a blessing to us and our children," Greg told us.

The Lernihans' stewardship journey isn't over, and they view wealth as a daily temptation. Marybeth said, "I realize that my identity can become tied to our money rather than to Christ. Greg keeps me centered when I fall into the temptations of this world, bringing me back to a focus on God and His kingdom rather than on worldly possessions." That raw honesty keeps Greg and Marybeth on the straight and narrow.

The Lord keeps surprising the Lernihans too. Greg said, "I always heard that you can't out-give God, and we've found that to be true. The Lord keeps giving us more opportunities to be generous."

Their parents laid a firm foundation on which Greg and Marybeth continue to build. They've become teachers and role models for so many people—like us—who aspire to live out our faith with everything we have, including our financial resources.

God Also Loves Addition

We don't want to make the mistake of honoring investing above charitable giving—and as we've seen in the Lernihans' story, they can fit together very nicely. God loves multiplication *and* addition. Think of Jesus's story of the shepherd who left the ninety-nine sheep to search for the one that was lost. It may sound crazy to jeopardize the welfare of so many just to rescue the one, but God loves individuals *and* the crowd. Sure, He wants to multiply His kingdom, but He does it by adding individuals.

God's upside-down kingdom puts the first last and the last first. The apostle Paul wrote that "God chose the foolish things of the world to shame the wise; God chose the weak things of the world to shame the strong. God chose the lowly things of this world and the despised things—and the things that are not—to nullify the things that are" (1 Corinthians 1:27–28). The powerless and the voiceless are near to the heart of God. Sometimes, He turns the game of addition into the game of multiplication, but sometimes He doesn't.

Dana was living in India during graduate school studies at Jawaharlal Nehru University when she met Mother Teresa, spending a couple of days volunteering with her in Calcutta, one day working with lepers and another day with orphans. Born in Albania as Anjezë Gonxhe Bojaxhiu, Mother Teresa wasn't strategizing about how to rise to worldwide fame when she founded the Missionaries of Charity to care for the sick and dying in India. She was called to care for those with no hope and no future—people who could give nothing back to her but their gratitude. If today we didn't know her story, her service to God would be no less potent and precious. There are undoubtedly countless Mother Teresas whose names we'll never know but who daily engage in the game of addition.

Author Mary Ann Evans, known by her pen name George Eliot, wrote in her novel *Middlemarch* that many good things in the world are "partly dependent on unhistoric acts; and that things are not so ill with you and me as they might have been, is half owing to the number who lived faithfully a hidden life, and rest in unvisited tombs."[20]

When we serve who Os Guinness calls "the Audience of One,"[21] our strategic planning should always take a backseat to God's specific call on our lives. There are many people of world-class talent working in preschools and warehouses and driving trucks because they have obeyed the Lord's calling. World-famous Olympic runner Eric Liddell left behind fame and fortune in Scotland to be a missionary in rural China, eventually dying in a Japanese prison camp in 1945. His last words were, "It's complete surrender," referring to his life lived unto God.

John and Sara Bolin, Jon Porter, and Greg and Mary-beth Lernihan each demonstrate in their own ways that God loves profit when it's justly earned and rightly deployed. He loves charitable grants, and He loves investments in businesses that produce human flourishing. He loves nonprofits and for-profits. He loves it when we turn the few talents He's given us into many more through our ingenuity and hard work. He loves missions and business—neither more than the other. He loves to see business employed as an agent of prosperity. He loves the dignity that comes from profitable work. And He loves it when the first willingly become the last on behalf of the powerless.

God loves addition and multiplication.

Giving vs. Investing

Having first gained all you can, and, secondly saved all you can, then give all you can.

—John Wesley, "The Use of Money" sermon

Show me how you can give away enough money to end poverty. You can't. You need a bigger lens that thinks about your investment dollars to lift people out of poverty—a stewardship lens, not just a charity lens.

—David Simms, founder of Talanton

David Simms: From Charity to Investment

"Growing up, my nickname was 'Senator Simms' because everyone assumed I'd serve in Congress," said David Simms.

As the high school valedictorian, David had a bright future. His success as an Ivy League undergraduate student earned him a place in the vaunted Phi Beta Kappa honor society. Then, he moved on to earn two graduate degrees—one from Harvard Law and another from Harvard Business School.

People who do these things usually go on to earn a lot of money.

A *lot* of money.

But over the last twenty-five years, David has chosen a career path with a financially downward trajectory. After starting at Bain & Company (he was hired by Mitt Romney) and then working at the senior executive VP level for a national bank, David has repeatedly taken jobs that earn less and less money—"six or seven very significant pay cuts," he said. "I knew the Lord would provide, and God didn't put me on earth to chase dollars."

Obviously, David is very gifted. He's a brainiac with a penchant for business. But David has decided to use his prodigious talents on behalf of the poor. To say that's rare among David's classmates would be an understatement. In fact, he is the only Harvard Business School graduate from his section to have worked for a nonprofit that helps the global poor.

In 1984, David joined a trip to Guatemala and Costa Rica that was organized by Opportunity International, a nonprofit that provides financial resources and training to people in developing nations. There, he saw the enormous difference small loans can make to women entrepreneurs who then had the money to send their kids to school and give them a ticket out of poverty.

During the Great Depression, David's dad had dropped out after eighth grade to get a job and help his family. That prevented him from moving ahead financially. "But I had an amazing education, and I learned firsthand the importance of education in overcoming poverty," David said. "The only time I saw my Irish immigrant father cry was when I graduated from the University of Pennsylvania."

In 2000, David was inspired by entrepreneur and author Bob Buford's challenge to develop a life mission statement. "Mine was 'to be a Christian venture philanthropist, mobilizing resources to help lift people out of poverty in Christ's name,'" David told us. "And my definition of success has been clear for a long time: I want to someday hear God say, 'Well done, good and faithful servant.'"

With those twin visions, David set out to start something that had never been done before: build a Christian organization that uses investment capital to support values-aligned, growth-stage businesses in the developing world to provide well-paying jobs for the poor. David had worked in microfinance at Opportunity International, but he had become convinced that microloans to the poor, while stabilizing life for people, didn't lift them fully out of poverty. "The lack of an economic updraft was the big issue for me. The missing economic engine needed for growth was catalyzing small- and medium-sized enterprises in the developing world, businesses much larger than the microfinance sector serves," David said.

Thus was born Talanton, which has now raised more than $30 million in personal and donor-advised fund capital to invest in East African businesses, most run by Christians according to Christian principles—companies like Masaka Farms in Rwanda, founded by entrepreneur Jon Porter (see chapter 4). And David has big dreams to grow the assets under management to $100 million or even a half billion, creating thousands of dignifying and empowering jobs for Africa's poor. "My passion is turning every dollar into jobs, and to exceed 250,000 jobs by the end of this decade," he said. "Scale and multiplication with the hope of the gospel are key to combating extreme poverty."

David believes that alleviating—and preventing—poverty requires more than charity; it also requires investments in businesses.

When we met David in 2016 and heard his vision, the Lord had prepared us to come on board right away. We had been looking for ways to invest in businesses in the developing world as a more sustainable intervention for poverty prevention, but we didn't know how we could vet companies half a world away. David Simms and Talanton filled in that gap.

Financially, David could be in a much different place today had he followed the well-worn path trodden by many of his Harvard classmates. "Do I have regrets?" he mused. "No. I look at my colleagues from business school—several of whom have become CEOs of Fortune 500 companies—and yet many have deep regrets for how they have lived their lives. They realized too late they weren't pursuing the right things. I had different priorities."

We expect David will get his wish and someday hear the Lord say, "Well done, My good and faithful servant."

The Limitations of Giving

Tithing and giving to nonprofits are beautiful things that reflect God's heart. They reflect His mercy expressed through the gift of God's only Son. When we give away something valuable, we relinquish control and transfer a measure of our power to someone else. Giving reflects the dying to self to which God calls us. Jesus said, "It is more blessed to give than to receive" (Acts 20:35).

However, David Simms's story reminds us charitable giving has limitations. For one thing, nonprofits are on a hamster wheel in pursuit of more contributions, devoting considerable time and resources—and sometimes appealing to fear or guilt—to solicit new donations. Economic downturns often depress charitable giving and throw nonprofits into a cost-cutting mode at precisely the time when demands on their work increase. The pool of US charitable capital is a zero-sum game with nonprofits competing against one another for scarce donors. Year-over-year charitable giving has been growing on average 6 percent each year for more than fifty years, but the percentage of people giving has shrunk steadily, with less than half of all households making even one charitable donation a year.[22] This means there is a shrinking pot of donors, making for fierce competition among charities.

> Economic downturns often depress charitable giving and throw nonprofits into a cost-cutting mode at precisely the time when demands on their work increase.

Charitable giving creates an awkward power imbalance for wealthy Americans who visit slums in the developing world. Our kids were deeply uncomfortable when we first took them into a Dominican Republic slum to visit the Compassion International project that hosted a child we sponsored. We, in our stylish clothes and pale skin and with our fancy Range Rover transport, shyly interacted with people who knew we were there to distribute money. We didn't know how to act in those settings, at least not in the beginning. Over time, we've gotten better at it, but it can feel voyeuristic for the givers and disempowering for the recipients.

Counterintuitively, giving can sometimes mar relationships. When Dana volunteered to serve Thanksgiving meals at a local shelter, the homeless people acted demanding and ungrateful for the free meal they were receiving. It was humiliating for many of them to be so dependent, and acting like they were impatient diners at a fine restaurant helped them cope with the indignity of their need. Far from forging a bond, giving can drive people apart.

In a broken world, it seems, even something as beautiful as a gift can be poorly given or poorly received.

Most people's limited experience has led them to view charitable giving as the only viable option for addressing human needs. However, as we'll see in the life of Aimee Minnich, it's possible to provide for others' needs without ever "giving" them anything.

Aimee Minnich: Using Charitable Capital to Invest in For-Profit Businesses

Aimee Minnich was an academic superstar. A National Merit Scholar who graduated summa cum laude with a major in philosophy, Aimee was working at Starbucks "along with a bunch of art history majors," she says with her characteristically dry wit. The question was what to do with the rest of her life.

Aimee knew what she *didn't* want to do: "For my whole life, people were telling me that I should become a lawyer. That sounded terrible to me! Nobody likes lawyers, and I didn't want to become one."

So goes the old joke: What do you call a cruise ship of lawyers that sinks?

A good start.

Or, as William Shakespeare famously wrote in *Henry VI*, "The first thing we do, let's kill all the lawyers."

On a whim, Aimee took the law school standardized entrance exam. She nailed it, resulting in a full ride from the University of Kansas Law School. Reluctantly, Aimee changed her mind and completed a law degree. She went to work at a law firm, helping businesses through mergers and acquisitions, but she told us, "I didn't like power or money enough to make this work. I needed to do something different."

Aimee was inspired by St. Irenaeus of Lyons' quote: "The glory of God is man fully alive."[23]

She remembers thinking, *Generosity is one of the ways we become more fully alive. If I can be a part of that for the rest of my life, that sounds pretty cool.*

That strong desire for deeper meaning led her to leave her law firm and take a position with the National Christian Foundation (a donor-advised fund), which equips Christians to be more generous. This was work that made Aimee's heart beat faster.

This was just the beginning. Aimee used her creativity and legal skills to dream up a way to leverage charitable giving for maximum effect: she and her colleague Jeff Johns imagined setting up a donor-advised fund dedicated to helping givers *invest* their charitable capital for economic, social, and spiritual transformation. Thus, Impact Foundation was born.

Since its founding in 2015, Impact Foundation has deployed more than $600 million in 606 companies worldwide and created more than seventy thousand jobs in companies run according to Christian principles.

One of the businesses in which Impact Foundation has invested is Hybrid Social Solutions, which provides remote Philippine villages that are beyond the reach of the electrical grid with sustainable access to high-quality, affordable solar technologies aimed at spurring economic development. This for-profit business founded by Harvard Business School graduate and Philippine native Jim Ayala has brought light and electricity to more than four thousand villages and improved energy access to 675,000 people over ten years. This access to power is revolutionary to people like food vendor Nanay Melita, who no longer has to travel hours for electricity access. Now, Nanay can keep her mobile phone charged, enabling her to stay in touch with her children in Manila. Reliable energy powered by the sun is transformative in the lives of the poor.

Hybrid Social Solutions is using the power of the marketplace to light up the lives of Filipinos in a way that would require millions of dollars in donations if a nonprofit organization were trying to meet this need. Plus, Hybrid Social Solutions does it while still providing financial returns to its investors. As we've demonstrated a few times already, for-profit solutions usually have broader reach, longer sustainability, and deeper impact to many vexing problems associated with grinding poverty.

"Impact investing is the future of philanthropy," Aimee told us. "Charity alone is not getting it done. The best intentions of philanthropy often hurt." Aimee contrasted the market-driven growth she saw in China with the perpetual poverty in Haiti that seemed to be impervious to the $13 billion in charitable donations that reached the small country from 2011 to 2021.

Launching Impact Foundation required the miraculous: getting an IRS agent to approve their application to employ their creative way of using charitable capital. As Aimee waited for what she was told would take many months, she began praying for the IRS agent by name, leaving her a voicemail every day. One day, the Lord gave

Aimee a vision to ask the agent to pick up their application, open it, and stamp it. Aimee immediately called the agent, who picked up the phone and told Aimee, "I just picked up your file. Hang on. I'm going to walk this down the hall to my boss." Minutes later, the application was approved, and Impact Foundation was in business.

Since that fateful day in 2015, Aimee sees her role as helping people who are stewarding a lot of resources to deploy their wealth on behalf of the world's materially and spiritually needy. She projects Impact Foundation will have $1 billion in assets under management by 2026.

The Lord is the one who empowered Aimee to use her impressive intellect to get a law degree that would unlock the legal hurdles to deploying hundreds of millions of charitable dollars for dire needs worldwide. For Aimee, all work done unto the Lord is worship. She is insistent that it's the Holy Spirit who fills up her cup. Unless she remains in the Lord, she doesn't believe her work will be effective: "We've got to remain in Him. It's from the overflow of the Holy Spirit in our lives that the Lord can do good things through us."

What Is a Donor-Advised Fund?

When we first heard about using charitable dollars to invest in for-profit businesses, our first reaction was, "That can't be legal." Thankfully, it is. Aimee Minnich is leading the way in directing charitable dollars into investments in for-profit businesses like those financed by David Simms at Talanton.

Let's get technical about donor-advised funds, or DAFs. A DAF is a nonprofit entity that receives charitable donations that are put into an account under the name of the donor. The donor is then permitted to advise the DAF on how the funds in their account will be donated or invested. A donor can select the companies in which they want to invest—and in the case of Impact Foundation, the business's social and/or spiritual impact must align with Christian principles. Later, when the donor's investments become liquid (i.e., available for withdrawal), they can invest in another company or grant the money to another charity. This process of investment and reinvestment can go on indefinitely, effectively multiplying the impact of the initial capital many times over before finally being granted to a nonprofit.

Most people just write a check to a charity using their after-tax earnings. But using a donor-advised fund has many advantages over traditional giving. As we've just seen, it holds the potential to vastly expand the impact of a charitable dollar. It's also convenient. If you give to multiple charities in a year, you will receive many tax-deduction receipts, but with a DAF you will receive just one receipt for your annual tax-deductible contribution and can quickly and easily designate charities to receive grants with just a few keystrokes, often in under one minute. And there's another advantage: You can choose to give anonymously from your DAF. The nonprofit can receive a check from the DAF without identifying which fund it came from. Given some recent incidents in which large donors' contributions were made public through illegal disclosures by disgruntled IRS employees, a DAF is one safe and easy way to protect your identity.

DAFs also give you the option to invest your charitable contributions before they're granted to a charity. Some funds, like National Christian Foundation, provide several investment options in faith-driven or traditional funds of publicly traded equities, bonds, or fixed-interest vehicles. If you prefer a traditional S&P 500 fund, you can choose that; or if you intend to keep your funds in the DAF for a brief time before directing them to a charity, you can choose a safer, low-interest option. The DAF will charge you a monthly fee for managing the fund, but we think it's very reasonable, not to mention worth it.

At one point, we explored setting up our own foundation, but when we compared it to a DAF, we couldn't think of any benefits to a foundation. A DAF has no requirements for quarterly meetings, no recordkeeping, no minimum distributions, and no tax filings. Plus, the DAF at National Christian Foundation will ensure that after we've died and some of the remaining funds go to our kids' DAFs, the funds will be constrained to charities consistent with NCF's values—something we've often seen go awry with foundations that begin contributing to causes that would have been inimical to their founders' vision. We've designated a list of charities that will receive funds in our DAF after we've gone home to be with the Lord. We update the list once a year to ensure we're still committed to the same nonprofits.

Private Investing with Charitable Capital

Early in our marriage, we began setting aside money in a separate savings account that we called "God's Fund"—our own unofficial and embryonic foundation. Dana thinks the best job in the world would be to run a foundation, and even when we were barely making ends meet with minimal savings, she had a vision for building a family foundation. In the early years, we had just a few hundred dollars in it, but over time, it's grown considerably—especially as we've been steadily increasing our tithe well beyond 10 percent.

Once we learned about National Christian Foundation, we transferred the money in God's Fund to our donor-advised fund and called it Oakton Foundation (since we live in the town of Oakton). We had created our own "foundation" in keeping with Dana's long-held dream, with a minimal monthly cost and enormous benefits. Initially, our intent was to grant all the money to nonprofits, but in recent years we've become enthusiastic investors in private businesses in the United States and internationally (especially Africa) that are run according to biblical principles, treat their employees well, and provide goods or services that contribute to human flourishing. The investments in our DAF at Impact Foundation run the gamut from Jon Porter's Masaka Farms in Rwanda (see Jon's story in chapter 4), to an organic pesticide company in Kenya, to an orchard in Mozambique.

The investments are usually tied up for several years, so they are not available or liquid like money in a stock fund. But it's incredibly exciting to know we're helping to launch and grow companies in frontier markets where capital is scarce and extremely expensive. We've become convinced that the poor in developing countries want to learn to fish more than they need a fish, and the businesses in which we invest are providing middle-class jobs paying fair wages and valuable products for consumers. If these businesses are successful, our DAF will have all the investment returned with interest, and we'll be able to replicate the process with a new business—the goose that lays the golden eggs again and again. If the business fails, at least people will have been employed for the duration of the company's life, and they will have gained valuable work experience they can take with them.

We like thinking about all the people in Africa who are gainfully employed, providing food, clothing, shelter, health care, and education to their families because of their jobs in small- and medium-sized enterprises (SMEs) we invest in. We both love to "nerd out" and do the math to determine the number of people who have jobs today thanks to our DAF investments. This puts a spring in our steps as we earn money to give away. These businesses are, in turn, providing numerous "downstream" jobs to suppliers, building up the much-needed "missing middle"—those middle-class jobs in mid-sized businesses that are prevalent in healthy economies but lacking in most of the developing world. These jobs often do far more to lift up the poor and prevent future poverty than a nonprofit could ever do.

We know clean water is vitally needed in the developing world, and we respect and admire people committed to helping poor communities get access to clean water. But our calling is to provide the capital for the businesses that will hire workers who can then afford to address their need for clean water without their ever feeling beholden to rich

Westerners providing handouts. The workers rightly consider they've traded their labor for their wages, and they've earned their pay—which is far more dignifying for everyone involved. This virtuous cycle of investments leading to businesses leading to jobs and profit leading to repaid capital with interest is a potent antidote to the crushing poverty afflicting the developing world. We couldn't be more enthusiastic about the small role we can play in catalyzing it through the charitable capital in our donor-advised fund. This is integral to God's call on our lives.

We would be remiss not to mention another way to help the poor: savings groups. We in the West take for granted the ease of getting a loan, whether by using our credit card or applying for a car or home equity loan. Capital flows freely, at least to those with acceptable credit ratings. Not so in the developing world, where the poor have no access to capital. Savings groups have emerged as a creative way to bridge this gap. These small groups of neighbors agree to save together and offer each other loans to start or grow a business. Five Talents (https://fivetalents.org/; Dana serves on this nonprofit's board) has found that the savings groups they helped launch have a 95 percent average repayment rate.

While we've been explaining how to use DAF accounts to do impact investing (investing with the goal of achieving both financial returns alongside social, spiritual, or environmental benefits), it's worth noting that the same can be done with private investable capital. We do impact investing inside and outside our DAF because we want all our capital to align with our faith in Christ.

No Ill-Gotten Gains

When we explain to other people our passion for impact investing, we often hear that such investments are risky and will likely result in lower returns than standard market indices like S&P 500 funds. That may well be true—or maybe not. Time will tell. But we are willing to forgo a percentage of returns if it means our faith and capital are better aligned. We also don't want to seek the highest investment returns if it means compromising our faith. Maybe strip clubs are providing handsome returns to some investors, but we want no ill-gotten gains. The Lord doesn't call us to set up a brothel to fund missionaries!

Thankfully, we don't believe we have to choose between market-based returns and faith-aligned investing. There are more than 250 funds in the United States that are consciously seeking to align biblical values with financial returns—and we expect more to form as demand increases. There's evidence that the stocks of businesses run by faith-driven CEOs who create healthy cultures for their employees outperform the market, which makes sense: treating employees well contributes to employees who treat customers well, which then benefits company shareholders. We believe following biblical principles generally leads to more prosperous and healthier businesses.[24]

To align our faith in Christ with our investing, we seek to employ both negative screens and positive screens. Negative screens are not going to be the same for everyone; one person may decline to invest in alcohol companies since their profit margin may come from alcoholics, whereas another person may see alcohol as a good gift of God that can rightly be enjoyed in moderation. There are few bright lines as to what Christians may or may not invest in (that which exploits or abuses people or violates their fundamental human rights is one bright line), but that doesn't mean we should pay no attention to the companies in which we invest. To the contrary, living a life of self-examination is central to following Jesus, and that should include where we put our money.

> Living a life of self-examination
> is central to following Jesus,
> and that should include where
> we put our money.

We love the way the nonprofit Praxis (www.praxislabs .org) explains positive screens in two layers: ethical and redemptive. The ethical screen ensures that a business doesn't harm anyone or anything, plays by the rules, solves problems, and adds value. The redemptive screen is "creative restoration through sacrifice—to bless others, renew culture, and give of ourselves. Redemptive actors pursue an 'I sacrifice, we win' approach with the agency and resources available to them. The motivating force behind the redemptive way is fundamentally other-centered: to love and serve."[25] This approach provides a good framework for investing with a "redemptive edge."

It's not necessary to quit your day job to become a full-time business analyst in order to figure out which investments align with your faith. When Dana was first confronted with the prospect of having to "look under the hood" of our investments, she was terrified. She contemplated having to do research on every public company to figure out who was exploiting workers—and that was time neither of us had. In recent years, a plethora of organizations and resources has sprung up to help faith-driven investors make God-honoring decisions (which we spell out in appendix B).

Not everyone can control all their investments. For instance, many company-based 401(k) retirement plans provide a limited number of broad-based market funds. It's important not to let the perfect be the enemy of the good. After Dana overcame her fear, we began a methodical review of our investments, and we have been making changes to more closely express our faith in our financial resources. For instance, we changed from one credit union to another that catered to a Christian membership and was focused on providing loans to churches. It's not that we thought our previous credit union was doing anything wrong, but the new credit union is providing us with a double bottom line in that we are receiving market-based interest rates even as churches are receiving mortgages at fair rates.

To be clear, what we're describing is not just for the wealthy. Most people have some assets they're managing, even if it's just a bank account and a retirement account. Aligning your faith in Christ and your money is hardly a radical concept—it's just too little discussed in the church (which is why we wrote this book). You don't have to do it alone. Get a financial advisor who shares your faith and can help you navigate what may otherwise be a daunting terrain.

The Rutt Family: Building the Kingdom

Jeff Rutt and his married daughter Alisa Hoober are from Bill's hometown in Lancaster, Pennsylvania. Alisa shared with us, "When I was in elementary school, my parents invited my siblings and me to make presentations about where our family should be giving money. I didn't think it was weird; that's just what we did. Looking back twenty-five years later, I realize how unusual that was." Alisa's kids are now doing the same thing.

This culture of giving was knitted into the family fabric by Alisa's parents. Jeff got it from his father, whom he remembers sewing up holes in the fingers of his gloves on Saturday and then dropping a big check in the church offering plate on Sunday. "I thought that was normal," Jeff said.

It would be an understatement to say that Jeff Rutt has been fabulously successful. In 1992, Jeff grew weary of the relentless time commitment required for his three hundred dairy cattle, so he sold the farm and became a homebuilder. Within fourteen years, Keystone Custom Homes was building three hundred and fifty homes annually. They became the first company in the country to win America's Best Builder Award three times.

It would be easy for the Rutts to live in one of the large, luxurious homes Jeff builds for others. Instead, Jeff drives a sixteen-year-old Toyota Camry with 329,000 miles on it, and they live in a hundred-year-old farmhouse. "But we're doing fine. We are grateful to be experiencing all the truly good things in life," Jeff assures us.

Instead of building a huge empire to hand on to Alisa and her siblings, the Rutts have given away 89 percent ownership of Keystone, which has $400 million in annual revenue, to the National Christian Foundation (NCF), using the profits to spread the gospel worldwide—addressing both spiritual and physical needs. Jeff credits his idea to give away most of the value of Keystone Custom Homes to the example of Alan Barnhart, who gave Barnhart Crane & Rigging to NCF. Alisa sent her dad the video of Alan's story, and Jeff decided to reach out to find out if the story was legit.

"When Alan picked up our president at the airport in his old car and took him to his humble home before sending him off a day later with a $1 million check for our ministry, I knew he was for real," Jeff told us. "Alan was transparent and clear about his journey, and our objectives were exactly the same: we were both looking to produce profit for purpose in the most efficient, effective way possible."

We asked Alisa whether she was upset to see her inheritance given away. Not in the least, she said. "We never felt like the business was our family's—it always belonged to the Lord. Gifting most of it to NCF felt very natural," Alisa said. "My parents are so frugal and so generous. I never felt wealthy growing up. The Wesley principle described my parents so well: Earn all you can to save all you can to give all you can. We were taught to be content with what we have."

Jeff's passion for world missions dates to his teens when he stood up at a church meeting to oppose paving the stone parking lot when that money could be better spent on missions. "I probably sounded like a rebel kid with a crazy idea," Jeff muses today. But this was just the beginning of Jeff's zeal to use resources to advance God's kingdom.

As their wealth grew, the Rutts were sending containers of food and medical supplies to churches in Ukraine. It was well intended, but it inadvertently created that cycle of anticipation, expectation, entitlement, and dependency.

"The Ukrainian pastor told us, 'Your helping is hurting.' That one comment shifted our whole approach," Jeff told us—and this was fifteen years before Steve Corbett and Brian Fikkert would author the influential book *When Helping Hurts*. In response, the Rutts founded HOPE International in 1997, providing biblically based training, savings services, and loans that restore dignity and break the cycle of poverty.

"We didn't know anything about Christ-centered enterprise, but we knew we wanted to get away from 'toxic charity,'" Jeff said, referencing the Robert Lupton book by the same name.

Jeff speaks fondly about when HOPE International gave a loan for a clothing store to Nadia from Ukraine, who then expanded her business into selling cement. Nadia paid off her loan with the proud proclamation, "I won't be needing any more loans because I'm not poor anymore."

Two Muslim women in Kigali, Rwanda, expanded their tiny sneaker business with a HOPE loan, and they later came to Christ by the witness of their loan officer.

Anastasia in Burundi couldn't afford to send her two daughters to school, and she leveraged a $20 loan into a successful wedding business. She and her business are thriving.

The Rutts founded HOPE in 1997 with funds generated on the same principle as the loans they make: They donated apartment buildings worth $1 million that generated rental income for HOPE. They also ask other homebuilders to sell homes from which the net proceeds go to HOPE. With the help of CEO Peter Greer (profiled in chapter 8), HOPE's work worldwide has exploded with more than $1.7 billion in loans to entrepreneurs.

Jeff and Sue are eager to pass on to their children wisdom, not wealth. And they have done that in spades for Alisa and her siblings Ben Rutt and Leah Barber. Alisa told us, "We were spared from the dangers of wealth thanks to how our parents raised us. We have lots of open conversations about money. We have more than enough money, and our focus is about how we can do more, leveraging the gifts we've been given. We want to steward our gifts and our story to encourage others to do more too. Christ is so generous with us, and we get to be generous with others."

Asked to sum up his approach to life, Jeff quickly replies, "Faithful steps following God's leading and praying through each part of the journey, trusting He has what's best for us in mind." Those good words find ample expression through the Rutts' many acts of generosity and stewardship.

Without a doubt, the Rutts are building their generational houses on the Rock.

God loves charity, and He loves investments. Both have important roles to play in advancing the kingdom of God, but the church has focused on the former and neglected the latter. Giving can be a beautiful thing, though it has limitations that can be overcome with for-profit investments. David Simms, Aimee Minnich, and Jeff Rutt have demonstrated how to use for-profit investments to empower the poor while providing nonexploitive and dignified work. Giving and investing are both valuable tools in addressing human needs, and we shouldn't disparage either one.

The Sanctifying Role of Work

We are called to stand in for God here in the world, exercising stewardship over the rest of creation in his place as his vice regents. We share in doing the things that God has done in creation—bringing order out of chaos, creatively building a civilization out of the material of physical and human nature, caring for all that God has made. This is a major part of what we were created to be. . . . Work has dignity because it is something that God does and because we do it in God's place, as his representatives.

—Timothy J. Keller, *Every Good Endeavor*

Pete and Deb Ochs: Working to Change Lives

Seventy percent of prisoners in the United States will return to prison within five years of their release.[26] It's a sad statistic, and it's the highest in the world. Contrast that with a select group of former inmates at the Hutchinson Correctional Facility in Kansas. Those inmates who worked for the in-prison Seat King manufacturing company during their incarceration have an astonishing 7 percent recidivism rate—that's 90 percent below the national average.

This tremendous success wouldn't have happened if Pete Ochs, founder of the private equity firm that started Seat King, had followed his original plan to be an orthodontist. After taking a finance course in his junior year of college, Pete quickly realized God created him to use his skills in business.

"I'm an entrepreneur by birth," Pete told us. When he wasn't working long hours on the farm as a boy, he was building lemonade stands or rockets—anything he could do to exercise his creative gifts. Upon graduation from the University of Kansas, he spent seven years in commercial banking, but that didn't scratch his entrepreneurial itch, so Pete started a private equity firm at age thirty. Over the next decade, the business began to grow and prosper, creating a new dilemma for Pete: What should he do with the profit from this new venture?

"Deb [Pete's wife] and I both grew up in homes that were very generous. We wanted to carry on that legacy," he said. "I was focused on growing my wealth as much as possible so that my 10 percent tithe could be big." But he didn't consider whether God had designs on the other 90 percent of his income too.

Understanding that he wasn't an owner but a steward "totally changed my approach to business and investing,"

Pete told us. "I thought stewardship was financial generosity, but then I came to realize He really wanted *me*, not my money." Pete learned the purpose of business was to glorify God by catalyzing human flourishing. Business was no longer just an engine to generate profits to be given to churches and charities but a thing that was pleasing to God in its own right.

This changed mindset had dramatic consequences for what businesses Pete invested in and how the businesses were run. "Previously, I didn't want to give my employees raises so I could make more money so I could give more money away," he said. "When I came to understand that stewardship and investing is more holistic in nature, I came to see capital via spiritual, economic, and social lenses."

The businesses themselves have been the means of bringing people to the Lord—even more than some of the ministries Pete supports with his charitable capital. Pete's design is to create great relationships inside the company and with customers, helping them to see the fruits of a changed life in Christ.

Before Pete's private equity firm buys a business, he asks four questions:

1. Does it honor God?
2. Does it serve people?
3. Can we do it with excellence?
4. Are we being good stewards of God's resources?

If a business checks all four boxes, then Pete and his partners move forward.

During his four decades in business, Pete has invested in and operated companies in the energy, manufacturing, banking, and education sectors, often in places devoid of human flourishing such as poverty-stricken countries and prisons. He's now running businesses in two prisons that employ two hundred and fifty inmates and rely on another one thousand employees in Mexico. Pete pays prevailing market wages to the residents of the prison so they have a decent job, which means they can impact their families and society in a positive way. The employees pay 25 percent of their gross wages back to the prison for room and board, and combined with the exceptionally low recidivism rate, the prison businesses are saving the state of Kansas millions of dollars. Plus, Pete found that the better he treats his team members, no matter who they are or what they've done in the past, the more profitable his companies become.

"The inmates who work for us at the prison have committed some of the worst crimes. We have a big vision for our guys—to have the best prison in the US," Pete said. The transformation extends well beyond the financial. The employees participate in Bible studies, life coaching, and classes on fathering and financial stewardship. The business also matches dollar-for-dollar what the employees voluntarily give to a list of designated charities—often helping the victims of the crimes they committed.

The men also help one another. One of the employees ran up to Pete recently and said, "Pete, my mom's house burned down, and she had no insurance. Within twenty-four hours, my fellow inmates had raised $11,500 for my mom!" His business is turning men who once had no hope into workers, savers, and, most importantly, *givers*.

Pete readily recognizes there's a cost to being generous, but it's an investment he believes will return much greater rewards. Pete and Deb capped their lifestyle twenty-five years ago after being challenged with the question, "How much is enough?" He will tell you that it is probably the best decision they have made as they have been front-row witnesses to God's miracles.

When we asked Pete what he's been learning in the last years, he was quick to say, "I need to surrender. Leading, managing, and stewarding are what we do, but surrendering to the lordship of Christ is about listening and asking what the Lord wants of me."

> "Leading, managing, and stewarding are what we do, but surrendering to the lordship of Christ is about listening and asking what the Lord wants of me."

Pete and Deb's surrender is freeing people from spiritual and financial bondage and transforming the world. They're multiplying their returns in heaven by forgoing some luxuries in this life, and our world is also a little richer for it. While a career spent aligning crooked teeth is a noble one, Pete answered a different call and has spent himself aligning his businesses with the kingdom of God.

Made to Work

In 1982, Loverboy had a hit single, "Working for the Week-end." The premise of the song was the opposite of the biblical vision of work and something foreign to Pete Ochs. The biblical vision is that we rest in order to work rather than working in order to rest. The principle of multiplication— and profit—begins with our labor. Adam and Eve were instructed to cultivate the garden to add value to the raw materials God provides.

Dana started working at a fast-food joint in Englewood, Colorado, at age fifteen. Bill also began working at the same age when he got his first job as a dishwasher at a diner in Lancaster, Pennsylvania. We both experienced the thrill of going to work and the joy of receiving a paycheck. There was a sense of dignity in work. Almost fifty years later, this is still true. (Bill works at a law firm, and Dana works for Impact Foundation.)

We both come from German stock, and a high work ethic is part of our mutual ethnic heritage. We work hard and long. We believe work is our calling—not just for workaholics or people who love their jobs, but for everyone. We were made to work. In Genesis, God commands the first humans to maintain the garden and have dominion over creation—and this was before humanity's rebellion and fall. A rhythm of six days of work and one day of rest is at the heart of creation.

The rebellion brought the thorns—metaphorical and literal—that made work more arduous, but that didn't relieve us of our call to work. Paul wrote in Colossians 3:23–24,

"Whatever you do, work at it with all your heart, as working for the Lord, not for human masters, since you know that you will receive an inheritance from the Lord as a reward. It is the Lord Christ you are serving."

Recall Jesus's story about the rich man who built bigger barns to accommodate his bumper crop. There's nothing wrong with bigger barns in themselves; the problem was the farmer did it so he could stop working and take it easy. But the Lord said to him, "You fool! This very night your life will be demanded from you. Then who will get what you have prepared for yourself?" (Luke 12:20). The sin was in both his sloth and his hoarding.

Retirement?

These verses should be scary to some people who view their retirement as the end of the race. Our rest comes in heaven, not in retirement. Until then, we are commanded to work. Why? Because to bear God's image is to create and build. Work is a large part of what it means to be human. We will work even in heaven. Author Randy Alcorn writes, "Because work began before sin and the Curse, and because God, who is without sin, is a worker, we should assume human beings will work on the New Earth. We'll have satisfying and enriching work that we can't wait to get back to, work that'll never be drudgery."[27] If you're in a job that you hate, it might sound great to be without work. But if you think of the most satisfying work you've ever done, you'll get a glimpse of what it will be like in heaven.

We have friends who are beginning to retire. They've run the numbers, and they believe they have enough money to live out their lives without paid work. Good for them . . . maybe. We say "maybe" because if retirement means a time to kick back and pursue a life of leisure and self-indulgence, that's contrary to the scriptural mandate to work. This may sound like sacrilege to the American Dream, but our current retirement culture seems out of step with the biblical vision. One study has also found that retiring early may even shorten your life![28]

On the other hand, there is a danger of idolizing work and ignoring God's command to rest. Too many Christians seem to think there are only nine commandments that still apply, that the Sabbath was an Old Testament thing. Not so. Jesus sought to reform antihuman Sabbath observance by doing away with legalistic rules, but He affirmed the importance of Sabbath rest. We shouldn't be workaholics.

Observing the Sabbath has been a part of Bill's Christian life since his first job as a dishwasher—a job he was ultimately fired from because he wouldn't work Sunday mornings. Bill observed the Sabbath through college and graduate school—and even on Capitol Hill and in the White House. It can be hard to do, but the Lord knows we need rest.

But the rest is so we can work, not the other way around. People who work hard for their career so they can enjoy "golden years" of hobbies, sunning, travel, and a perfect lawn have perverted the relationship between rest and work. Rest is a cessation of our usual work precisely so we are better equipped to work again. That's part of the reason a sedentary office worker's Sabbath may look different than a carpenter's—what constitutes rest may look different for each of us. The key is that we're ceasing work to focus on God and recharge our batteries. Think of the Sabbath as a time to sharpen the saw so we are equipped to serve.

And to be clear, work doesn't have to result in a paycheck. Perhaps you've spent your career in the classroom, and your retirement is doing volunteer work at your church or hospital or civic center. The key is that we are serving others through our work, paid or not. Bill's father spent the last year of his life in assisted living during COVID. He told Bill he wondered why he was still alive at eighty-eight years old with little discernible purpose, but Bill told him that everyone who entered his room was another person to whom he could minister. Our words of encouragement and admonition and instruction are a form of work, pleasing to the Lord when done for Him.

We have met many exemplars through our participation in the global "generosity community" who are dedicating their time and talent toward intentional kingdom-building endeavors in what would normally be their retirement years. The creativity, enthusiasm, meaning, and joy that they experience is contagious! "Retirement" should represent the *redeployment* of our resources, skills, and service, not the end of it.

Scott Friesen: Work So Others Might Live

Scott Friesen's teenage daughter asked, "Dad, do you have a dream house?" Scott thought for a minute, and then said,

"Yes, and I've seen it. It's on the ridge overlooking Lake Austin." The house has a patio and pool, and it sits high atop a ridge overlooking downtown Austin, Texas. There's a path down to the lake with a dock for a motorboat.

"Can we afford it, Dad?" asked Scott's daughter. Scott replied, "We can afford it, but we believe God's called us to live simply and use our money to build businesses that create jobs in Africa."

When Scott was in high school in North Carolina, he dreamed of being a millionaire by age thirty. "It wasn't so much the lifestyle," he says now at age fifty-two, "but the significance and respect that I craved. I figured if I were a millionaire then I'd really have value as a human." Scott grew up in an upper-middle-class home, so he wasn't in *need*; he was more in *want*. He wanted to be self-sufficient.

As a business major at UNC-Chapel Hill, Scott worked on the side, not because he needed to—his commercial airline pilot father was paying the tuition—but so he could have his own money and continue his illusion of self-sufficiency. Though he was led to the Lord as a child by his dad, Scott had a deeper encounter with Jesus in college. It started when a campus minister told Scott that his desire to meet every student on campus was vain. "At first I was offended," Scott said, "but over the weeks, I reflected on that comment and realized it was true."

As his relationship with the Lord deepened, Scott's desire to be a millionaire by thirty receded. Instead of going into business after graduation, Scott became a campus minister with InterVarsity. But after five years, the Lord led Scott into business after all, and he found out he was good at it.

"I was the guy who knew how to take an idea and build a business around it," he told us. By age forty-one, after building and then selling businesses three times, Scott was a multimillionaire and no longer needed to work. Spiritually, he had matured beyond his youthful desire to get rich to prove his significance. Scott and his wife, Karen, were living below their means, and they weren't flaunting their new-found wealth—aside from the Audi S-7 that Scott describes as "ridiculously fast." Scott said, "To preserve my life, I traded it in for a F-150 pickup truck after a couple years."

Initially, Scott's plan was to become a full-time philan-thropist, serving on nonprofit boards and playing plenty of golf on the side. But a trip to Ethiopia in 2013 to visit one of the charities he supported got his entrepreneurial juices flowing. "I saw tons of great business opportuni-ties there—opportunities to help people by creating jobs through for-profit businesses and opportunities to make money for investors," he said. "That trip gave me a vision for God's call for the second half of my life—to use my experiences as an entrepreneur to build large-scale, for-profit businesses in Africa that would create thousands of decent, life-changing jobs."

Several years earlier, Scott had been struck by an important truth in Scripture: "Anyone who has been steal-ing must steal no longer, but must work, doing something useful with their own hands, that they may have something to share with those in need" (Ephesians 4:28). Scott had come by his wealth honestly, but now as a wealthy man who could pursue a life of leisure until the end of his days, Scott had a new vision for using his money. He wanted to employ it not for his own ego or comfort but to share with those in need. In his words, "I am called to work so that others may live. I turned away from what looked like a rich life to a high-wire act in Africa that could potentially deplete my wealth."

Instead of managing their wealth to ensure he wouldn't *need* to work again, Scott and Karen (who was a willing and eager partner every step of the way) deployed their money in high-risk/high-reward ventures in East Africa. "Our financial advisor counseled us to preserve our core wealth and just put a small fraction into our businesses in Africa, but we didn't do that. We gave up some of our financial security to do this business. Sometimes that feels very costly. That decision was my 'God commanded Abraham to sacrifice Isaac' moment," Scott said.

First with a medical device company, then with a string of business start-ups from beef production to orchards to diplomatic housing to high tech, Scott has used his wealth on behalf of "the least of these" in his aptly named "Verdant Frontiers"—making frontier markets *verdant*, or lush with new growth. He's invited other investors to join his work and has created a portfolio of over $180 million in assets in Africa, providing thousands of good jobs for employees and suppliers. Scott's vision is to fight poverty and create human flourishing through business.

Scott wants to both lift Africans out of poverty through productive work and attract more capital investments into

Africa by providing market-rate returns (or better), demonstrating that the investments aren't "concessionary." Profits are at the heart of Scott's mission because they're the engine that can change the continent for the better. "I want the Wall Street bros to come into Africa because they can make money there. Market-based returns will produce market-based transformation that's sustainable and transformative," he said.

Scott's original ambition for Verdant Frontiers was for the business to directly create a 1 percent increase in Ethiopia's GDP, but now he's got a bigger dream: to create one hundred thousand life-changing jobs in Africa. That's ambitious, and he may never get there. But we suspect the Lord is pleased with Scott striving for wealth creation that sustainably lifts up economically disadvantaged people.

Scott's dream of becoming a millionaire has come true, but what he's done with those millions is vastly different from the independence he envisioned as a high school student. "Leading Verdant has been the hardest thing I've done in my life, and it's been the best thing. I'm not a traditional CEO, and the work has shown me in thousands of ways and experiences how much my work and my life depend on the Lord."

The Idolatry of Leisure

Scott's example demonstrates the joy of continuing to work and empowering others to work. But there are also practical reasons why too much rest can be bad for us. The Lord commanded that we rest one day and work six days, in part because not working enough can make us self-centered, self-indulgent, and cranky. We may develop a tendency to gripe about trivial things that mostly escaped our attention during our years of paid work. We can become connoisseurs of the frivolous when our job becomes our next leisure activity. There is a fine line between feasting and gluttony, resting and sloth. Counterintuitively, we enjoy rest far more when it's only a punctuation in our work. When it becomes our main thing, it loses its luster.

> We enjoy rest far more when it's only a punctuation in our work. When it becomes our main thing, it loses its luster.

Our lives are more responsibilities to steward well than gifts to be enjoyed. God made us to serve Him and serve others, and not primarily so we could have happy lives. Whether or not we're happy is far less important than whether we are responsible with the resources—time, talent, and treasure—with which we've been entrusted. None of it is ours to own; it belongs to God, and we will be called to give account for how we use the Lord's resources.

For those who have concluded they no longer need to work for pay because they have saved enough money, why not follow Scott Friesen's example by continuing to earn money and then give it all away?

The worldwide median family income is $2,920.[29] Yes, that's $2,920 *per year*, or $243 per month. If you're making the US median household income of $74,000,[30] imagine what your after-tax earnings could do in the lives of the world's poor! If your net pay is about $53,000, you could double the median income for sixty-two families. Or consider how that money could be used to scale small- and medium-sized businesses in the developing world, creating a perpetual motion machine of wealth creation for middle-class jobs that transform families and economies. And then do that for five years—years you otherwise might have spent on your hobbies. Instead, you are transforming the lives of thousands of people for generations to come! We in the developed world are uniquely equipped to reduce poverty through our paid work. And for high-net-worth people, that power increases exponentially.

At this point, you might be thinking we've become a bit too "judgy." But we're just raising questions for you to take to the Lord. It's between you and God. We're not your judge; He is. The question is whether the normal course of retiring and spending a couple of decades in pursuit of leisure is the Lord's call for you. When Paul was facing the prospect of his execution at the hands of Roman authorities, he relished the thought of finishing his life and being with the Lord. But then he went on to revel in the thought of living, as "this will mean fruitful labor for me" (Philippians 1:22). We are called to fruitful labor always, whether in chains (as Paul was when he wrote to the Philippians), in a job we don't love, or in retirement from paid work.

Can You Afford to Stop Earning Money?

There's also the question of whether we've earned enough money to stop working. This requires careful planning, including for the unexpected.

Bill:

> *My father was fantastic in almost every way, but when it came to planning for his financial future, not so much. He presumed the government or his family would care for him in later years, so he stopped working at age sixty-two. When he ran out of money, my siblings and I stepped in. We were grateful for his years of faithful parenting with our mom, but my dad could have done a better job planning so he wouldn't need his kids' financial support.*

Hoarding is wrong. James inveighed against the rich who "hoarded wealth in the last days," living "on earth in luxury and self-indulgence" (James 5:3, 5). Yet Proverbs 6 adjures us to emulate the ant that stores up provisions for the future. The line between hoarding and responsible saving may not be clear, but it's one for which we should aim.

On a practical level, if you're unsure whether you're hoarding, you can cap the wealth you're leaving to your family upon your death and designate nonprofits that will receive your posthumous gifts. This way, you can avoid becoming a financial burden to your family without hoarding wealth. We use the National Christian Foundation's succession planning tool. We've capped how much money goes to our kids (on an inflation-adjusted basis).

The balance will go to our donor-advised funds, and we've designated several charities that will receive funds upon our death.

By God's grace and inspired by the example of others in this book, we've reached our finish line and no longer need to earn money to support ourselves—but that doesn't mean it's time to "retire"! Instead, we're transitioning into giving away all our take-home pay and exponentially increasing our giving to our donor-advised fund. Bill daydreams about how much money goes to ministries for every day he works. When he's having a difficult day due to tensions at work, he remembers the good his earnings are doing for a poor family in East Africa, and it helps alleviate the stress of the moment. Bill could be one of the world's fifty million slaves. Instead, he's in a well-paying job that is empowering him to transform the lives of thousands of people through his earnings. That puts a spring in his step!

As you're considering whether you should retire from paid work, consider these practical questions:

1. Why do I want to leave my paid work? To get away from an unpleasant job? To spend all day by the pool? To enhance my service to the Lord in a new chapter?

2. Have I saved enough money to responsibly stop earning an income?

3. Is my spouse in agreement? The Lord often directs us through our spouses.

4. What will my new work be? Will it occupy most of my week in fruitful service?

5. Would I serve better by continuing my paid work and giving away my net income?

6. How will I maintain my self-discipline without an employer? How will I fight sloth and self-indulgence?

7. Who will hold me accountable for the use of my time and money?

Richard Okello: Working His Way out of Africa . . . and Back Again

You might mistake Richard Okello for Friedrich Nietzsche's "Ubermensch" or "Superman," considering how hard he works. Richard has known adversity and powered through one challenge after another. But unlike Nietzsche's ideal human, whose goal is to usurp the role of God, Richard lives under God's authority.

"Unstoppable" would be another fitting word to describe Richard. Growing up in Uganda, he was a natural-born leader. "I've been leading as long as I can remember," Richard told us. "I even remember some bad things I did in kindergarten when I led other kids to do bad things too."

In time, his leadership skills were turned to good, including helping lead a five-year campaign at his private boarding school to abolish caning, upending the school's monopolistic bakery by setting up a rival bakery that charged fair prices, and being picked to attend an exclusive boarding school in Wales with a full scholarship in recognition of his leadership qualities.

Through a providential meeting with the dean of admissions at Swarthmore College, Richard made his way to this prestigious and demanding college in the Philadelphia suburbs, working the night shift on the campus shuttle while carrying extra class credits per semester so he could graduate with honors in just three years.

Richard's biological mother died during his freshman year, leaving him the responsibility of financially supporting his three stepsisters in Uganda. He secured well-paying positions as a teacher's assistant and at a think tank in the summer to cover his and his family's needs.

Richard knew how to make money in every situation, in part because he was a relentless and talented worker. "There were instances when I could have been forgiven for taking credit for my success, but not in the totality—it was so obviously God's intervention in my life," Richard said. "God in His mercy would not let me think that I was the reason for my success because of the downfall that can often bring."

Upon graduating, Richard was given a plum position at the vaunted Bridgewater Capital, working for the legendary Ray Dalio. Within five years, Richard had become a partner—a meteoric rise by any standard. At Bridgewater, Richard learned important lessons that remain with him to this day. Bridgewater's premium on radical candor "only works for people who are willing to look at their own weaknesses and strive for self-improvement," Richard told us. They also had a motto of "excellence at all costs." At one point, Richard was responsible for a $30 billion client business unit.

In 2011, Richard decided to leave the comforts of Silicon Valley and return to Africa to start Sango Capital, an investment management firm focused on delivering superior risk-adjusted returns from investments in Africa. "The idea of Sango Capital started before I even left Africa," Richard told us. "I grew up during a time of rapid change in Africa, and later saw classmates who had been underachievers in middle and high school do very well for themselves pursuing innovative solutions to basic problems in the region." Richard had an opportunity to bring lessons learned from Bridgewater to help shape a fast-growing industry in the last investment frontier in the world.

Richard maintains that Africa is an overlooked investment opportunity. Sango Capital's website notes impressive statistics about the financial potential in Africa:

- $2.1 trillion in household consumption by 2023
- A burgeoning population headed to 1.5 billion by 2030
- An expectation that Africa will add more than 400 million people to the global labor pool over the next decade, most of whom will live in its fast-growing cities and be tech-savvy
- $3.5 trillion in business-to-business consumption demand by 2025

Sango Capital is thriving and attracting significant investment from US institutional investors, most of whom had never invested in the region before and who believe in the team's ability to identify, grow, and exit attractive business opportunities. Richard uses that capital to back management teams of fast-growing companies that, in turn, provide quality jobs for fellow Africans. He waxes eloquent about the major advantage that private capital has over International Monetary Fund loans or other development capital. It's this potential that drives Richard to steward the enormous talent the Lord has given him on behalf of a continent ignored by many.

Along the way, Richard has been blessed with a wife of over twenty years and two energetic teenagers. He leans on God to help him navigate the increasingly challenging terrain of parenting. "You have to redefine difficult things as things that should get done now, and impossible things as challenges that will just take a little longer," Richard said. "Because of God's mercies in my life, I have come to see things differently than other people. It should have been impossible for me as a university student to help raise my siblings." But he did.

Richard is leading the way in using his prodigious talents on behalf of "the least of these," helping lift fellow Africans who lack opportunity through work that brings dignity and deep satisfaction—instead of dependency-generating handouts.

We were made to be productive, whether paid or unpaid. Even when we rest, it's principally to equip us to work. Work done to the Lord—from trash collection to accounting to software engineering—pleases Him, blesses others, and blesses us. Work usually produces fruitfulness, multiplying God's resources by combining our labor with God's good gifts to bring prosperity. Before we fall into the well-worn retirement trap and become grumpy, self-indulgent old cranks, we should bear in mind Paul's admonition to the Corinthians:

> Do you not know that in a race all the runners run, but only one gets the prize? Run in such a way as to get the prize. Everyone who competes in the games goes into strict training. They do it to get a crown that will not last, but we do it to get a crown that will last forever. Therefore I do not run like someone running aimlessly; I do not fight like a boxer beating the air. No, I strike a blow to my body and make it my slave so that after I have preached to others, I myself will not be disqualified for the prize. (1 Corinthians 9:24–27)

One reason we wrote this book is to encourage Christ-followers to consider thinking more intentionally about how they personally might play a role in the universal church prayer "Your kingdom come": God could raise up the very rocks to usher in His plan to repair that which is broken, but it's more keeping with His designs to have His people rising up to bring redemptive solutions to global problems.

The Dangers of Money

> Where I have known one man fail through poverty, I have known fifty men fail through riches.
> —Charles Spurgeon

Don Simmons: Radical in Disguise

Don Simmons is countercultural—many call him *radical*—but Don considers himself as simply being obedient. He looks every inch the part of a financial advisor: He's sensibly dressed, has a conservative hairstyle, and wears studious glasses. On the outside, perhaps the only remarkable thing about Don is the 1948 seaplane he loves to fly. But what's inside is a different story.

"My wife, Amy, and I are seeking to deploy all our resources for kingdom purposes before we die," Don told us. "We've been steadily shrinking our lifestyle." The Simmonses sold the 6,500-square-foot home they loved to move into a 2,400-square-foot home more in line with the median house value in the United States. "It's been very freeing to simplify our lives," Don explains. "Most of my clients, due to a fear of running out of money, die with more than they could ever spend. We are choosing to reduce our lifestyle earlier than most people, so that our resources can be deployed to bring the salt and light of the gospel to unreached people, now."

For the first half of his career, his investing philosophy was squarely in line with the mainstream: seek to maximize financial returns for clients. Period. But then Don discovered the concept of "business as mission"—namely, that not just charitable donations but investment in for-profit business could be used to deliberately and proactively advance God's kingdom on earth, often more efficiently and effectively than purely charitable donations. Don pored over the Bible's many verses about wealth and concluded that the biblical view of investing is far different from the world's. This has led to personal changes in their investment portfolio and in how Don advises his clients.

"I had been taught that maximizing financial return was the most important thing. But God cares about multiple bottom lines, not just profit," Don explained to us. Don and Amy have 50 percent of their investments in businesses that are thoughtfully advancing the kingdom of God, and they are working to get to 100 percent. Don maintains that Christians have not yet created enough investment products to build a completely balanced asset-allocated investment portfolio. But this is changing, and Christian money managers are starting to think more strategically about

creating funds and alternative investments that seek positive eternal impact.

"It is my hope that ten years from now, Christians will
be able to invest in a well-balanced portfolio that achieves
both temporal financial goals and eternal outcomes simultaneously," Don said.

Don readily concedes that investing with multiple bottom lines can be riskier than focusing on profit alone. This,
he believes, is not his problem; it's God's. It's the Lord's
money to begin with, and Don doesn't want to invest it
in anything that runs counter to God's purposes for the
world. Don also believes this approach requires reevalu-
ating all investments—including home equity and retirement funds, which should also be used for missional and
redemptive businesses.

"Nothing should be invested for any other purpose,"
Don said.

This is a radical message, especially for a financial
planner. Some of Don's harshest critics are colleagues in
his profession. Yet Don isn't advising his clients to do any
differently than he is doing—or anything more than what
he believes the Bible requires. "We are not high-net-worth
people because we have been giving away our wealth about
as fast as it comes into our hands," Don said.

Choosing to serve full time without pay for a Christian
economic fund at age fifty (rather than continuing to grow
his practice and net worth) was another radical decision.
"I don't feel any sadness at not having more—but I am sad
when I see needs that I can't meet," Don added.

Don readily recognizes that Scripture doesn't prescribe a particular economic lifestyle. One person may live in a one-room house where another may faithfully serve the Lord while living in a mansion. Still, Don is concerned that most financially successful Christians have chosen a lifestyle many multiples above the median household income of $74,000[31]—which is still in the top 10 percent worldwide. "If Christians deployed more of their wealth, we could address so many more issues of global poverty," he said.

Don doesn't espouse a prosperity gospel of *giving to get*, but he states that "my experience has been that the more Amy and I have sacrificed, the more the Lord has put into our hands to deploy. He has blessed us so we can be generous on every occasion," he said.

Central to Don's calling is also challenging others to follow the biblical pattern for investing, which is why he wrote *The Steward Investor*. He argues we are fiduciaries who own nothing but manage everything to achieve redemptive objectives of God, the True Owner. Through his book and his business, Don would like to see $1 billion released for God's kingdom through missional enterprises over the next decade. "Donations are not sacred, and investments are not secular—our investments are just as sacred as the donations that we make when we're managing it all as God's fiduciary," Don said.[32]

Radicals, it turns out, come in all shapes and sizes— and some, like Don and Amy Simmons, are seeking to advance an upside-down vision for the world that puts profits in their proper place under the lordship of Christ.

Who's Wealthy?

Don Simmons knows the dangers of wealth and acts accordingly. But we've known people who are wealthy and won't even acknowledge it to themselves. Many people in the top 1 percent refer to billionaires as "those rich people," but they act as if they're not also wealthy. It's somehow offensive for people to refer to themselves as rich or even think of themselves in those terms. The same is true for most people in the West. If you're making $30,000 and supporting a family of four, you're in the top 74th percentile worldwide, and if you make the US household median income of $74,000, you're in the top 11th percentile worldwide.[33] But few people making each of those salaries *feel* rich, though they indisputably are rich from a global perspective.

There are good reasons for this. For one thing, we measure ourselves by people in our immediate proximity. Dana grew up in a wealthy family in an exclusive suburb of Denver, Colorado, but because she didn't have a butler or a Rolls-Royce like some of her friends, she thought she was middle class. She thought Bill was a guy from "the other side of the tracks," though his family earned more than twice the median household income.

We suspect there may be another reason many people shield themselves from recognizing their wealth. Perhaps you know Stan Lee's famous Peter Parker Principle from Spider-Man comic books: "With great power comes great responsibility." It's a variation of Jesus's words, "From everyone who has been given much, much will be demanded"

(Luke 12:48). The same is true of wealth, which is another form of power. Bill got to know Stan Lee, and he invited him to have breakfast in the West Wing of the White House when he was a special assistant to President George W. Bush. Bill talked to Stan about the Peter Parker Principle and lauded him for smuggling into popular entertainment such an important idea.

If we refuse to acknowledge the power and wealth we have, we might be able to absolve ourselves from the responsibilities that come with both. But if we fully acknowledge all that we've been given, we must also come to grips with our corresponding responsibilities. Even if you are truly among the world's poor (and if you are, you're unlikely to be reading this book since you couldn't afford to buy it or access it), you also have a responsibility to use whatever money you do have for God's glory. Jesus said, "Whoever can be trusted with very little can also be trusted with much, and whoever is dishonest with very little will also be dishonest with much" (Luke 16:10). In God's economy, what matters is being faithful with what we've been given, great or small.

In God's economy, what matters
is being faithful with what we've
been given, great or small.

Money: A Dangerous Blessing

Money is dangerous. The Bible is littered with warnings about money. For example, the Old Testament warns,

> When you have eaten and are satisfied, praise the LORD your God for the good land he has given you. Be careful that you do not forget the LORD your God, failing to observe his commands, his laws and his decrees that I am giving you this day. Otherwise, when you eat and are satisfied, when you build fine houses and settle down, and when your herds and flocks grow large and your silver and gold increase and all you have is multiplied, then your heart will become proud and you will forget the LORD your God, who brought you out of Egypt, out of the land of slavery. (Deuteronomy 8:10–14)

Similarly, in the New Testament, we see this warning from Paul to his ministry protégé Timothy:

> Those who want to get rich fall into temptation and a trap and into many foolish and harmful desires that plunge people into ruin and destruction. For the love of money is a root of all kinds of evil. Some people, eager for money, have wandered from the faith and pierced themselves with many griefs. (1 Timothy 6:9–10)

Note that Paul didn't say that *money* is the root of all evil, as it's often misquoted, but that the *love* of money is *a* root of *many* evil things.

Jesus likewise warned about "the deceitfulness of wealth" that chokes out faith (Matthew 13:22) and that it is easier for a camel to go through the eye of a needle than for a wealthy person to enter the kingdom of God (Matthew 19:24). Obviously, Jesus was being hyperbolic here as He often was when He wanted to communicate an important truth. (Think of all the blind men if Jesus really wanted people to gouge out their eyes when they lusted!)

Bill:

I—more than Dana—feel the love of money sometimes wrapping around my heart like a boa constrictor. During my morning devotions, I regularly uncoil that idolatrous love with my own liturgical prayer, which includes these words: "There's nothing that I have that's not from You; there's nothing I have that's not a gift."

What good things do we have that we can't trace to God? Our parents, our genes, our daily food, our friends—they all come from God. He who created literally everything *ex nihilo* (out of nothing) is responsible for the goodness we enjoy. Recognizing our gifting snuffs out any room for arrogance or boasting and plants us in the realm of gratitude—and gratitude is the secret ingredient in a life of joy.

Recognizing our gifting snuffs out any room for arrogance or boasting and plants us in the realm of gratitude.

We love quotes from wise people. We've got them stenciled on our walls and framed in our powder room. (To our utter delight, our then ten-year-old daughter recited unprompted many of the quotes she had memorized during her trips to the bathroom!) Among the quotes is one from Corrie ten Boom, the Dutch concentration camp survivor who was responsible for saving about eight hundred Jews from the gas chamber before the Nazis caught her: "Hold everything in your hands lightly, otherwise it hurts when God pries your fingers open."

Money is certainly one of those things to be held lightly.

We can think of many reasons that wealth can be dangerous:

Wealth Gives the Illusion of Control

As we saw in chapter 1, onetime billionaire Dennis Bakke said that wealth can give us the illusion of control. It's true that wealth gives us power to do things—and to prevent things from happening.

As our wealth has grown over the years, we often note how much easier life has become. Where we once stressed over the smallest expenditures, we can now take in stride car repairs and expensive plane tickets and nicer hotels. But as Paul reminds us, "wealth . . . is so uncertain" (1 Timothy 6:17). It's prudent to be grateful for what we have today and constantly remind ourselves that we may lose everything we have.

Wealth Can Make Us Greedy

We can be greedy for money whether we're impoverished or already millionaires. It's not wrong to want money to meet our needs and others'. But the fuzzy line between wanting money in an appropriate way versus a sinful and selfish way is discernible only in our hearts.

Dana:

> *I recognized I was prone to sin not only in my desire to save a lot of money but also in my strong inner need to "protect" our furnishings and assorted belongings from damage caused by houseguests. For years, I was hesitant to host friends in our home, because I was a bit . . . overly enthusiastic . . . about keeping our home free from the scratches and stains that come from hospitality. God has softened that greedy, overprotective part of me over the years, and I now accept those "love scars" as part of living in community. I must admit, though, that it took a while for me to allow God to fully heal and transform that selfish part of me. In fact, it was the result of eight years of confessing to and praying with my small group about my pattern of prioritizing material possessions over my relationships with other people.*

Wealth Can Make Us Lazy

As we saw in chapter 6, we were made to work, and when we use our wealth to "build bigger barns" and become self-indulgent, we sin. The book of Proverbs is full of condemnations against laziness not only because it can lead to poverty but also because it's selfish and can make us unsatisfied: "A sluggard's appetite is never filled, but the desires of the diligent are fully satisfied" (Proverbs 13:4). Laziness is one of the most respectable sins, lauded in advertising and cherished as the proper goal for retirees. But it's work, not laziness, that is more likely to lead to contentment.

Wealth Can Distract Us with Luxury

Wealth can make us comfort-seeking and addicted to luxuries. There is a time for comfort and luxury, but when they become lifestyles, we are in spiritual danger. Bill, who has been memorizing Scripture for more than forty years, recently finished James 5, which includes these stern words:

> Now listen, you rich people, weep and wail because of the misery that is coming on you. Your wealth has rotted, and moths have eaten your clothes. Your gold and silver are corroded. Their corrosion will testify against you and eat your flesh like fire. You have hoarded wealth in the last days. Look! The wages you failed to pay the workers who mowed your fields are crying out against you. The cries of the harvesters have reached the ears of the Lord Almighty. You have lived on earth in luxury and self-indulgence. You have fattened yourselves in the day of slaughter. You have condemned and murdered the innocent one, who was not opposing you. (James 5:1–6)

Yikes! Those words merit careful attention. But when is buying dinner at an expensive restaurant okay, and when is it wrong? Only God can answer that question as you seek His guidance, examine your heart, and listen to wise counsel from other Christ-followers. It's not only whether we *can* responsibly afford a luxury but also whether we *should* afford it—and how often we indulge.

When we bought a new house, Dana wrestled with whether it was okay to spend money on plantation shutters or whether metal blinds were sufficient. She sought out wisdom from others and prayed through her desire before she felt liberty to buy the shutters for the main floor (but only blinds for the top floor and the basement). Yet she purposely drives a thirteen-year-old van with a huge gash down the side from one of our kids hitting a mailbox. She feels no liberty to buy a new vehicle or to get the gash repaired. For someone else, the answers to these questions might have been totally reversed—we're not suggesting that what we thought we were supposed to do in these situations is what everyone should do. But we know at least this much: We shouldn't strive to envelop ourselves in as much luxury as we can afford.

Wealth Can Confuse Us About Ownership

Another danger of money is to believe it's ours. It's not; it all belongs to God. Job 41:11 says, "Everything under heaven belongs to me," and Psalm 50:12 says, "The world is mine, and all that is in it." Jesus's parable of the talents communicates that the master gave his money to the servants to manage—but it was still the master's money.

If we're owners, we can do whatever we want with the money, but if we're stewards of God's money and answerable to Him, how we use the money will likely be very different.

Wealth Can Make Us Arrogant

Bill:

I find it so easy to look at someone who has less wealth and quietly think arrogant thoughts. It's so ugly, and I know to repent when those vile thoughts cross my mind, but they seem to arise with some frequency.

We should not judge others. Don Simmons, whose story we used to open this chapter, has forsaken greater wealth and a larger house for the sake of the kingdom, but someone who didn't know this might think he's not particularly successful as a wealth advisor. Such arrogant thinking is incorrect and sinful. We can't know for sure whose financial success is due to personal excellence or hard work or thrift—plus, all those things come from God anyway. It's wrong to equate wealth with virtue or spiritual maturity.

Wealth Can Lead to Exploitation

Another danger of money is that it can make us prone to exploit others. Again, in James 5, the wealthy are condemned for hoarding wealth and failing to pay the field hands. Too often, wealth comes from exploitation of others. Maybe you can hire a worker at below-market wages, but that may be wrong. There are no bright lines or easy answers, but the questions must be posed inside our hearts. Ask the Lord whether you're being fair to your contractor or your landscaper or your mechanic. We are supposed to pay fair wages. Legally, you can get away without leaving a tip for your waiter, but it's not right.

Wealth Can Spoil Our Children

It's tempting to want to give our kids all the things we couldn't afford when we were growing up, but we might ruin them. Having unfulfilled desires is healthy, and getting everything we want can be dangerous. We have friends whose net worth is in the tens of millions of dollars but who limit how much money their kids have and how much will be left to them in inheritance. They are passing on to their kids the value of hard work and a legacy of generosity toward others.

If we treat money like fire, we're headed in the right direction: in its proper channel, it brings life, health, and joy. Outside its rightful boundaries, it can incinerate our souls. The next story is about someone who's seen many of the dangers of money expressed among her clients and her colleagues.

Rachel McDonough: Using Wealth as Intended

Rachel McDonough is fluent in two languages: wealth and poverty. She knows what it is to live in both—and she feels uniquely called to serve both the wealthy and the poor.

The daughter of missionaries, Rachel lived below the poverty level in the United States. She recalls receiving government-subsidized school lunches and her mother praying for money to buy milk. But her family was comparatively rich while living in Kenya. Being approached for handouts by the street kids in Nairobi as a ten-year-old was the first time she had to decide how she would respond to poverty. It left a big mark.

"The pain on their faces and knowing that they did nothing to deserve it changed me forever," she told us. "It was then that I began to understand that holding wealth not only gives us *opportunity* but also *responsibility*."

Back in the United States, Rachel saw herself as wealthy, even though by American standards her family was poor. This "bilingual" experience has had an enormous impact on her life. "I'm still wrestling with the question of my relationship to money," Rachel said.

Upon graduation from college, Rachel took a job as a receptionist at Merrill Lynch, worked her way up to a financial advisor role, and was immersed in the language of wealth. "Seeing many affluent clients struggling with a scarcity mentality or lack of clarity on the purpose of their wealth was eye-opening," Rachel told us. "God was giving me His heart to serve not only the poor but also those holding the wealth. I began to understand that it's difficult for the wealthy to know *how exactly* they will live out Micah 6:8—to act justly, love mercy, and walk humbly with your God."

Rachel attended a Kingdom Advisors conference in 2009 that changed everything. After hearing presentations on how stock investors were inadvertently profiting from addiction, slave labor in supply chains, and other objectionable business activities, Rachel was undone. "I went back to my hotel room and wept, repenting before the Lord," she told us. "Not only had I been naive about where the profits for my clients were coming from, but I had been complicit. For example, I had clients who were giving to pro-life causes and still had investments that supported and profited from the abortion industry."

For the next three years, Rachel continued as a financial advisor but with a deep-seated unease. She had a conviction about what needed to change but no idea how to integrate faith values into investment portfolio construction. A couple of years later, she attended the same conference again, searching for answers. One speaker, financial advisor Dan Hardt, shared candidly with the roomful of advisors about how he had told his Christian clients about the un-Christian things in which they were invested because of his past recommendations.

"I was taken by his authenticity, candor, and courage, and I knew that I was willing and able to have those same uncomfortable client conversations—if only I knew how to help them invest differently," Rachel said. As the session ended, she was silently praying that the Lord would send someone to show her the way and, in return, she bargained with God that she would pay it forward and help another advisor someday. Thirty seconds later Dan Hardt approached her, offering to have a series of phone calls with her.

Rachel began taking risks, such as offering to help a multimillionaire couple who were prospective clients align their investments with their faith values. "To my utter shock, they said yes!" Rachel told us. She completed a comprehensive research project for her new client that eventually became the foundation for the integration of faith and investing across her practice. She was blazing a trail where few had gone before.

Rachel has a passionate love for the Lord, and when she was praying for ways to bring Him gifts, she got an idea: share her newfound knowledge about faith-driven investing with other financial advisors. She reasoned, "If I could share what I've learned with a hundred financial advisors instead of just a hundred clients, I could multiply my impact." That's exactly what happened.

Since that time, Rachel has disseminated her expertise to more than one thousand financial advisors at no cost to them. "I just gave away the farm, not worrying about being compensated for my intellectual property," she said. She was boldly challenging the advisors to take the same risks she was taking with her clients. She even shared the gospel with some of her clients, reasoning, "As much as I enjoy having them as clients, I'd rather have them as neighbors in heaven." Her boldness has cost her some relationships, but she has great peace.

Rachel and her husband don't have as much money as they could have had, in part because they've chosen not to work full time in order to spend more time with their young children. Most of her generosity is expressed through an impact-first approach to her professional life, partnering with clients to redirect the flow of capital, writing, speaking on stewardship, and serving fellow advisors. But she also takes enormous joy in spontaneous generosity—like the time she felt led to approach the mother of a family of foster kids who were playing ball together in a public park, asking if she could write a check for $500 on the spot. The mother began to cry, saying she had just been praying for provisions.

Rachel insists that "it's essential that we learn how to listen to His voice and get in sync with the Holy Spirit hour by hour," which is exactly what she strives for and why she's been a trailblazing financial advisor, redirecting the flow of capital and inviting others to join her merry band.

"God knows no lack that He should be dependent on us to first multiply His wealth so that He might achieve His goals (especially not through exploitation of the vulnerable)," Rachel told us. "In fact, I don't believe God has *financial* goals at all. He instead has *relational* goals for our stewardship. Our heavenly Father uses our stewardship journey as a platform to teach us to think as He thinks and feel as He feels about humanity and the world we're called to cultivate and keep. Through our surrender, alignment, and faith, our stewardship decisions can pull down the culture of heaven into earth."

Faithfulness Doesn't Necessarily Lead to Prosperity

Rachel's story reminds us that wealth isn't a Christ-follower's goal. While it's true that God loves profit, wealth doesn't come to all of us. In fact, the Lord calls many Christians to become poor for the sake of the kingdom—like the rich young man whom Jesus called to give away all his money to the poor and to follow Him (Mark 10:17–31).

There's a strong tradition among some Christian leaders to say otherwise. They explicitly state that God wants all Christians to be rich. This teaching is dangerous and unbiblical. It's true that riches do come to some Christians, but that's up to the Lord to decide. Obviously, if you're poor because you refuse to work, that's a choice you're making. But many people have a strong work ethic and have no opportunity to become wealthy, like the many hard-working people we've seen on our trips to very poor countries in the global south.

Equating faithful living with prosperity ignores many important biblical teachings, makes people feel needlessly inadequate if they're not wealthy, and causes us to judge others who aren't blessed with many resources. It's dangerous to suggest that suffering is not part of our call as Christians. In Hebrews 11, there is a list of people who have succeeded by "conquering kingdoms" and others were "sawed in two." God decides our destiny, and whether we are rich or poor, powerful or despised is in the Lord's hands. Our job is to be faithful until we draw our last breath. What He does promise us when we give generously is that we "will abound in every good work" (2 Corinthians 9:8).

Our job is to be faithful until
we draw our last breath.

Not Divinizing Poverty

Just as we shouldn't consider wealth as a sign of our faithfulness, we shouldn't be holding up poverty as holier than wealth. Considering Jesus's admonition to the rich young ruler to give away all his wealth to the poor (Matthew 19:16–22), it's understandable why we might think that giving away everything is godlier. But Jesus's instruction was specific to that man, apparently because that was the one thing he was unwilling to give up. If Jesus had been talking to someone else, the admonition might have been to relinquish power, prestige, or pastime—anything that comes before God.

Still, most of us aren't called to intentional poverty. As evidence, Paul has pointed instructions for rich people—verses we regularly recite after analyzing our household budget:

> Command those who are rich in this present world not
> to be arrogant nor to put their hope in wealth, which is
> so uncertain, but to put their hope in God, who richly
> provides us with everything for our enjoyment. Command them to do good, to be rich in good deeds, and to
> be generous and willing to share. In this way they will
> lay up treasure for themselves as a firm foundation for
> the coming age, so that they may take hold of the life
> that is truly life. (1 Timothy 6:17–19)

The command is to live a life of generous living, not impoverished living. Notably, Paul even says that riches are given to us "for our enjoyment." We shouldn't feel guilty about using the Lord's resources for fun things—in Bill's case sailing, and in Dana's case travel. Instead, we should give thanks for His rich provision. That's not to say we can spend money however we want, but it does mean the Lord delights in our using His resources in life-giving ways.

The challenge is to hold in tension two important truths: God loves profit and money, yet whether we are called to live with a lot or a little is up to Him. We are in no position to judge others for being rich or poor since there is not a one-to-one correlation between our net worth and our faithfulness to God. We should not be arrogant if we're wealthy, nor should we be jealous of the rich if we're poor. Each of us has a different calling, and we have no more basis to measure ourselves or others by our relative wealth than we do by our attractiveness, physical strength, or any other superficial metric.

Ask yourself, *Is there anything I would refuse to give away if the Lord asked me to?* If so, that's a strong indication that something other than God is on the throne of your heart. We'll see in this next story a couple who keeps money in its rightful place and has avoided its dangerous lure to seek comfort above faithfulness.

Curt and Katrina Aitken-Laird: Using Money Without Idolizing It

Curt and Katrina Aitken-Laird live bold and exciting lives. They casually told us they were each on a hit list when they were living and working in Afghanistan. Far too many of their friends were assassinated. They said it with a mixture of still-present grief and acceptance that a life of abundant purpose can also be marked with loss and hardship.

The Aitken-Lairds have known prosperity and wildly successful business ventures, and they've known poverty. At one time, they lived on a basic diet of canned tomato soup and food donated by friends, while a metal crate packed with snow served as their refrigerator. Again, this was mentioned as an aside, because it's reflective of the fabric of their risk-taking lives rather than being singularly important. But they were quick to add, "The privilege of our birth and our passports has always meant we have the option to leave and have family who will catch us . . . something we're so aware that our Afghan and African friends don't have."

This risk-taking extends to their finances too. "Stewardship entails interrogating our mindsets to make sure we're not holding on to our money or our talents. God owns it all," they told us. Curt and Katrina have resolved to go wherever the Lord leads. Currently, they live in Nairobi, Kenya. Next year, who knows!

Between them, the Aitken-Lairds have lived in fifteen countries and traveled to a hundred more. Each has lived most of their life outside their country of origin. Katrina's father is British, and her mother is Finnish. Curt's parents were American missionaries on the island of New Guinea, where Katrina's parents were public health doctors.

Many Americans live in dread fear that God will call them to move to an impoverished country. Katrina had the opposite problem. When she was living in Washington, DC, Katrina sensed God posing this question: "If I asked you, would you stay in the United States?"

Katrina replied, "Anything but that, Lord."

It's not that Katrina is anti-American; she just always saw herself in the developing world. She wrestled with God and finally submitted to His will. In the end, she sensed the Lord telling her, "I don't mind which path you choose, but what I care about is that you're going to walk that path with Me." With that, Katrina resolved to move to Afghanistan, which was being rebuilt in the wake of the American invasion.

Curt was already in Afghanistan, successfully building the nationwide mobile telephone company that would eventually be valued at $1 billion. He and Katrina met at church—a building later destroyed by the Taliban. Katrina had blonde hair down to her waist and a ring in her nose, rode a horse over mountains to deliver aid, met with warlords, and wore stiletto black boots that seemed out of place in the muddy terrain. Curt was immediately smitten. It took six years until they finally became a couple and married soon thereafter. They describe their marriage as "arranged by God for His kingdom purposes." And that's exactly how they're being used.

This couple that clearly adores each other eventually left Afghanistan after launching multiple successful business and philanthropic enterprises, moving to Nigeria and then to Kenya. Currently, they are building ReFrontier, both a nonprofit foundation and a for-profit fund that invests in a dense network of businesses run by Kenyans according to kingdom principles. They have a passion for elevating the poor and marginalized in frontier markets. Curt said, "We want to be yeast that leavens the indigenous strengths in a culture. Eventually, the yeast disappears, which is what must happen to us."

Their lives of generosity and trust reflect God's love of philanthropy *and* business. Katrina's expertise in nonprofit approaches to international development and Curt's entrepreneurial acumen combine in a hybrid way of addressing poverty alleviation and human flourishing all too rare among Christians.

Curt told us that "God is asking us to give Him our talents—and all we are. If your gifting is business, use your business skills for His glory. He wants your entire life. He can take it all away at any time—as He's done with us a couple of times." Hardship isn't necessarily an indication we're on the wrong path. Katrina said that "when the Lord gives you direction, you continue no matter how hard it gets—until you're given a new direction." The Aitken-Lairds' lives match their words as they tackle seemingly impossible assignments in dangerous places.

Katrina readily admits that she wrestles with God: "I love the verse, 'I believe; help me in my unbelief.' I wrestle with fear, and I long for the anchor and stability of a home. But I *choose* to be obedient, not that it looks pretty all the time. We may never get wealthy, and we may not even survive. But we'd never trade the richness of using God's gifts and laying them at His feet."

The Aitken-Lairds believe the gospel is like water—it will find the smallest crack. They are laboring to make those cracks in the parched earth so the Holy Spirit can do His work.

Some people spend their lives trying to avoid risk, but this couple embraces it—not because they have a death wish but because their love of God and His people, and their confidence in His character, compel them to follow God with reckless abandon. They told us, "We are not cavalier with our lives or finances, nor are we completely free of fear. But there's something better—a deeper love and a richer calling—that compels us to follow in obedience and that allows us to continue making peace with the risks that we feel called to make."

Andy Crouch, author of *Strong and Weak*, argues that "death is the last enemy not just because it takes life but because the fear of death prevents real life"[34]—another danger the Aitken-Lairds have avoided.

And that's precisely why they are truly alive, flourishing even in their setbacks. They love God more than their own lives.

Jesus and the New Testament writers warned about the dangers of the love of money and the deceitfulness of wealth. Given that most Americans are wealthy by almost any global standard, Christ-followers need to carefully balance striving for profits and wealth creation with the need to hold wealth loosely. The key is in seeing money as a responsibility, not something we own. Wealth is not a measure of God's pleasure with us or how godly we are. Many people worldwide are faithfully following the Lord in their poverty. The key is responsibly stewarding what God has given us for His glory.

Practical Steps to Steward Money

All the blessings we enjoy are Divine deposits, committed to our trust on this condition, that they should be dispensed for the benefit of our neighbors.

—John Calvin, *The Institutes of the Christian Religion*

How different our standard and Christ's. We ask how much a man *gives*. Christ asks, how much he *keeps*.

—Andrew Murray, *Money: Thoughts for God's Stewards*

Gisle Sorli: Managing Money for the Kingdom

Early in our marriage when money was tight, we drove thirty minutes to take our car to a mechanic whom we trusted implicitly. Distad's Amoco was a no-nonsense family business, and the mechanics would regularly save us money by telling us what services we didn't need and how to fix our car in the most economical way. When you find mechanics like that, you treasure them.

Gisle Sorli, a tall Norwegian immigrant who came to the United States to play soccer, is one such "mechanic"—except he's a financial advisor who encourages people to give away more money, which reduces how much money Gisle will earn in commissions.

"I was meeting with a couple in their sixties who had no kids and told me they wanted to spend all of their considerable wealth on themselves, playing golf all over the country for the rest of their lives," Gisle told us. "And that was a turning point for me. I was looking out my office window at the National Cathedral looming on the horizon, and I said to myself, *Is this how you want to spend your life—helping people live into their self-indulgence?*"

A couple of years earlier, Gisle had been certified as a Kingdom Advisor under Ron Blue's leadership, which had reoriented Gisle's thinking. Whereas some financial advisors seek to squeeze as much money as possible from their clients, Kingdom Advisors tutored Gisle to empower them to see how the Lord wants them to steward their money with a biblical worldview.

Gisle explained, "The main goal for most of my clients was financial independence—the total opposite of what God wants. He wants us to partner with Him in redeeming the world, and He wants us to be dependent on Him. He wants us to live in community with one another. I felt like I was leading people away from God's designs."

Gisle pulled together six godly friends to help him rethink his career. They concluded that Gisle should leave his firm and start his own business. He named it "Steward's Progress"—hearkening back to *Pilgrim's Progress* by John Bunyan. "I wanted to help families follow the Lord and avoid the world's traps. With my new business, I was in my sweet spot—helping people lean into stewardship of the Lord's resources."

For Gisle, success is more than just achieving financial returns; it's about encouraging people to be generous and to draw closer to God. This approach is unusual, even among many Christian financial advisors who are fearful they'll give up their earnings or lose their clients.

This hasn't been true for Gisle, but he wouldn't care even if it were. Gisle told us, "I'm not Mother Teresa: I'm making good money. My main goal isn't financial benefit but helping families get closer to God and have better relationships with others." Gisle never calculates how much more money he'd make if he didn't encourage people to be more generous. He gets enormous joy from seeing people find the freedom that comes from realizing they're stewards and not owners.

Gisle believes that stewardship involves much more than just giving away money. It also includes wisely investing capital in businesses that have multiple bottom-line returns—financial, spiritual, social, and environmental. This approach entails negative screens on investments— ensuring businesses aren't profiting by exploiting workers and trading in products that harm people or the world— as well as positive screens to provide a "redemptive edge."

This sometimes leads Gisle to encourage clients to invest in businesses that may provide lower financial returns—and therefore less money for him.

Gisle relishes the excitement he gets from his job, and he doesn't want to miss the privilege of leading people to be generous and to have their hearts softened to the Lord. He and his assistant pray for their clients and celebrate when they hear their clients are giving away more money.

There's nothing wrong with playing golf, but Gisle has found the joy that comes to him and his clients when they take a longer view of wealth—one that extends beyond this world "where moth and rust destroy and where thieves break in and steal" (Matthew 6:19 ESV).

Prudent Practices

Gisle's story reminds us that being a good steward requires effort, care, and attention. So far, we've been writing about principles. Now, it's time to get practical. What follows are things we've found helpful in working out our calling to steward what God has given us. These practical suggestions aren't new, and they're not comprehensive. We'll name specific organizations and tools we've used, but we're not pretending these are the only tools or even the best tools—they're just what's worked best for us.

Practice #1: Track Your Spending

As we mentioned in chapter 3, budgets can lie, but an accurate accounting of what we've actually spent tells the truth.

We recommend setting a plan for what you'll spend based on what you've been spending, because it's more likely to be realistic. Of course, you can always change your behavior if you've been spending too much money, but you should begin with the acknowledgment of what you've been doing and then determine to do things differently.

Too often, budgets fail to include unexpected things that should have been expected. If you spent $800 on "unexpected" car repairs last year, you should budget to spend that much again this year and then some, because your car is one year older. Hot water heaters will die, AC compressors will break down, pipes will burst, cavities will develop, and ACLs will tear. The second law of thermodynamics reminds us that things are coming apart. We're shortsighted if we don't build this into our budget.

Thirty years ago, we began using Quicken, which is one of several popular personal financial management software programs. It's worked great for us, aside from the occasional glitches attendant to all software. We've kept track of almost everything we've spent since then. All our expenses are assigned a category, so we could tell you how much we've spent eating out or heating our home or going on vacation. As crazy as it seems, our family has spent $70,000 dining out over the last thirty years. Gulp. That sounds like a lot, because it is! It averages out to about $50 a week. Now that we've written this down, we feel a bit embarrassed about it. But our annual and monthly budgets reflect that reality, and we know if we want to save more money we need to cut some expenses somewhere, and that might be our restaurant spending.

You could use Quicken like we do, one of the other excellent budgeting apps, a spreadsheet, or even a simple legal pad. Whichever method you prefer, the main thing is to keep track of your expenses. It's annoying and may feel like a cold shower, but it's part of what it means to live an *examined life* (Socrates said an unexamined life isn't worth living, and we think he's right). Once you have an accurate one-year record of everything you've spent, you're poised for greater success in your budgeting and living in reality—and you'll be equipped to make the necessary changes to be a better steward.

Another tool we've found to be invaluable is Crown Ministries (www.crown.org). They have videos, webinars, financial guides and calculators, counselors, and much more to help you begin your journey of financial stewardship. Our marriage has been remarkably short on conflicts about money because we're on the same page, fostered by immersing ourselves in Crown's teaching. Whether you're single or married, young or old, we heartily recommend Crown.

Practice #2: Save Money and Live Below Your Means

Americans aren't great savers. Many of us presume nothing will go wrong in the future, rely on credit, and live for today. But the path to good financial stewardship necessitates living below our means—in other words, spending less than we earn. It's not rocket science, but it is hard to do.

Albert Einstein purportedly said that compound interest is the eighth wonder of the world: "He who understands it, earns it. He who doesn't, pays it." To illustrate the power of saving money and then earning compound interest, consider the story of a girl who asked for just one penny from a miserly king during an economic depression. Even the king thought that request was too modest, so he encouraged the girl to ask for more. She then asked the king to double the pennies she was given the day before for a period of thirty days. Foolishly, the king granted the request. Thanks to the power of compounding, the girl who received just one penny on the first day of the month received $5.3 million on the thirtieth day.

The key is to start with one penny as soon as possible. This means beginning to save now. You might think you can't afford to save, but for most people, that's just not true. Pretend you didn't get a cost-of-living-adjustment and live on the same amount this year as you did last year and invest the balance. Or when you pay off your car loan, continue to save the same amount you were paying monthly—and then buy your next car without a loan. Shop at a budget grocery store or brew your own coffee at home. There are dozens of mental tricks we can play that will get us to the place of spending less than we earn. Each requires some measure of self-denial, but over time, they'll pay off big.

You might think you can't
afford to save, but for most
people, that's just not true.

Six years after we paid off our school loans, we found ourselves with one year's worth of earnings in the bank. It felt like a fortune as we were still relatively early in our marriage. We realized that if we'd taken one Caribbean vacation a year for each of those previous six years, we would have had no savings. Instead, we capitalized on the miracle of compound interest and accumulated a lot of savings. We experienced so much liberty from having savings—savings that was a huge source of comfort a couple of years later when Bill lost his job. We were facing unemployment with a generous cushion to take us through the drought.

We're not describing a life of asceticism. There are still times to enjoy luxury, but the key is learning to forgo at least some expenses for the sake of long-term financial gains. Self-denial is life-giving both in how we benefit years hence and in how it trains our souls today.

One of Bill's favorite Bible verses is 1 Peter 4:1–2: "Therefore, since Christ suffered in his body, arm yourselves also with the same attitude, because whoever suffers in the body is done with sin. As a result, they do not live the rest of their earthly lives for evil human desires, but rather for the will of God." If we can learn to begin the day with an "attitude of suffering," we can endure more self-denial and reap long-term and *very* long-term (a.k.a "eternal") benefits.

Practice #3: Beware of Debt

"The rich rule over the poor, and the borrower is slave to the lender" (Proverbs 22:7).

Debt is dangerous. It would be too strong to say that the Bible absolutely forbids debt, but it does discourage it and consistently warns how it can ensnare us. In a society drowning in debt, we think the American church is blind to this pervasive cultural failing. Christians often conform to the culture of debt, and we're the poorer for it.

Recent reports from the Federal Reserve Bank of New York show that credit card debt in America is increasing, with an average balance of $5,733 per cardholder.[35] With advertisers beckoning us to "obey your thirst" and "just do it," we're listening to the siren songs that lead to financial bondage.

We're not against credit cards. In fact, we put most of our monthly expenses on our card so we can get Amazon points to buy many things for free. But we pay off our credit cards automatically every month, and we've never paid one cent of interest. If you have the self-discipline to use a credit card well, they can be a huge blessing. If you lack the self-discipline, using a debit card is smarter. It's unwise to pay exorbitant credit card interest rates because you can't wait to buy something before having enough money in the bank to actually pay for it.

Education debt is a different story. Unlike consumer debt, taking on debt to get an advanced degree is likely to pay off in the long run—unless we fail to complete the degree and have nothing but debt to show for our efforts. It's also important to weigh cost-benefit ratios. It's unwise to take on enormous school debt so we can take a job that doesn't require a degree and won't pay enough to eventually enable us to pay off the debt.

Mortgages can also be sensible and entirely necessary for most people who want to escape endlessly paying rent without accruing equity. But we've found that whereas Realtors may push you to buy as much house as you can afford, a downturn in the market or unexpected job loss can quickly put borrowers "under water" (owing more than the house is worth) and struggling to pay the monthly mortgage.

We counsel people to put down a larger down payment to guard against market downturns or to maintain a healthy savings account that can continue to cover mortgage payments if the unexpected happens. Don't assume nothing will go wrong in the future; instead, build in ample safety nets. This may mean buying a smaller house than you'd like or staying in your current house for a longer time. Our family of five lived in a 1,600-square-foot townhouse for sixteen years. It was tight, but we found incredible freedom in having sufficient savings before buying a larger house for our growing family.

Finally, strive to be debt-free, even if that makes less financial sense to some people. It's true that you might be able to get better returns on your stocks than the interest you're paying on a mortgage or education loans, but there is a joy that comes from having no debt. It also equips you to move ahead fast when your income increases and you don't need the new margin to retire debt. Additionally, paying down your debt more quickly keeps you from having too much cash on hand that is tempting to use for frivolous purchases. Furthermore, limiting risk is an additional benefit of debt-free living. Aside from the joy of a paid-for house and car, you're also free of the worry of repossession and free from the burden of a significant monthly payment that you can redirect to other things.

Practice #4: Invest in Step with Your Faith

We should further the kingdom of God in everything we do, including our investing. The Lord wants us to do His things in His way.

We recognize how daunting this task can feel. We applaud all the do-it-yourself people in the world who fix their own cars and do their own plumbing, but few people are well equipped to do a better job—or even a more economical job—managing their own investments. Layer on to that the challenge of aligning your faith with your investments, and we think it makes good sense to partner with a financial advisor who's been certified by Kingdom Advisors, a Christian organization that trains certified financial planners to (1) integrate biblical wisdom into their financial counsel, (2) put clients' best interests above their own, (3) acknowledge that God owns everything and we are only stewards, and (4) commit to professional excellence.

The Lord wants His followers to be risk-takers—but not any and all risk. We're still called to be responsible, and finding the right balance between risk and responsibility is not a mathematical formula, though math may be involved in discernment. Get-rich-quick schemes can easily be mistaken for risk-taking, but they might be just foolish. Some people do pick the right stock or invest in the right start-up at just the right time and quickly make lots of money, but it's unwise to aim at such rare outcomes. It's wiser to think long-term about your investments. God cares about that "long obedience in the same direction" (oddly enough, a quote from Nietzsche), and this is no less true of our investment strategy. Market ups and downs come and go, but you're wise to keep your eyes on the horizon—both the long-term in this world and seeing into eternity.

When we began to align our investments with our faith, we did so step-by-step—and we're still doing so. You don't have to change everything in a single day. We started by looking at the stock funds we were in, and we began by employing a negative screen on certain businesses we think are unbiblical. Then, we moved on to employing a positive screen, using metrics and research done by respected Christian financial groups like Eventide (www .eventideinvestments.com) and Brightlight (https://www .brightlightimpact.us/).

We also invested some of the money at National Christian Foundation (our donor-advised fund) into Talanton (www .talantonllc.com), founded and led by David Simms, whom we profiled in chapter 5, which invests in values-driven, growth-stage businesses in low-income countries that create middle-class jobs—an approach we think is superior for alleviating and preventing poverty in the developing world. Talanton finds and vets these Christian-led companies run according to biblical principles, and they make affordable loans (and sometimes take an equity position) to grow these businesses, helping to nourish a flourishing middle class— something essential for creating the tide that lifts all boats.

Praxis (www.praxislabs.org) is "a venture-building eco-system advancing redemptive entrepreneurship, supporting founders, funders, and innovators motivated by their faith to address the major issues of our time." In the early days of our journey, Praxis was transformative in helping us see that God cares about everything, even our investments. The question we posed to Praxis was why the church hadn't been thinking about this before—a question without an easy answer. We think Praxis has helped unleash this fresh work of the Spirit to get Christ-followers to think more holistically about money and faith. We continue to joyfully attend their annual conference where we have found a community of like-minded people intent on aligning their faith with their capital.

Henry Kaestner's self-sacrificial vision in founding, funding, and building Faith Driven Investor (www.faithdriveninvestor.org), Faith Driven Entrepreneur (www.faithdrivenentrepreneur.org), and Solving the World's Greatest Problems (https://www.solvingtheworldsgreatestproblems.org/) has been nothing less than monumental in our lives. We geek out on their podcasts, go to their conferences, and participate in and then lead their "foundation groups" (online or in-person six-week studies that include inspiring videos and thoughtful conversation). It's one thing to hear a lecture about aligning faith and capital, but when we hear the stories of our fellow travelers, it's more powerful still.

We rely on two donor-advised funds—National Christian Foundation (www.ncfgiving.com, scaled up by David Wills, whose story is below) and Impact Foundation (www.impactfoundation.org), led by Aimee Minnich, whom we profiled in chapter 5—to help us deploy our charitable giving. We almost never write a check directly to a charitable organization. Instead, we contribute both cash and appreciated stocks and mutual fund shares into our donor-advised funds, thereby avoiding capital gains taxes. Then, we direct the DAF to send a check to the charitable organization in our name, or we invest the money in faith-driven public equity funds or groups like Talanton or even in individual businesses that operate according to biblical principles. These DAFs have been transformative in empowering us to be more creative and effective in our giving and investing, helping us to see the vital role of for-profit business in addressing many thorny problems.

We encourage generous-minded people of means to consider moving at least some of their charitable capital toward impact investing. Traditional charitable giving is fully democratized—anyone can donate any amount to a nonprofit. However, historically most impact investing has required a minimum of $25,000 per investment, often investing in early stage companies or risky environments.

> We encourage generous-minded people of means to consider moving at least some of their charitable capital toward impact investing.

Thankfully, there are platforms and companies democratizing access to this kind of investment. In 2015, the Securities and Exchange Commission opened up angel investing to nonaccredited investors (meaning you don't have to have a high income or net worth). Equity crowd-funding sites such as WeFunder and Start Engine allow anyone to purchase equity in a company for as little as $100. Additionally, some groups provide access to investors who write small checks through pooled investment vehicles. However, the majority of entrepreneurs seeking angel funding are typically seeking $10,000 minimum per investor, and more typically $25,000 to $50,000.

Another reason to move more of your generosity toward impact investing is evident in the chart in chapter 4—there is simply more money available in that "pocket." If Christians move more money into faith-driven instruments, the market will pay attention, financial advisors will create more faith-driven instruments, and a positive flywheel effect begins.

Practice #5: Walk with Others

We've found incredible joy—and challenges—in hearing people's stories about how they steward their resources. When we first attended The Gathering (www.thegathering .com), a conference for Christian philanthropists, we were most excited to have candid conversations with fellow attendees who were wrestling with how to use their finances to glorify the Lord. It was liberating to discuss details about our financial situation and hear others do the same. There was no sense of boastfulness or jealousy since it was as if we were at a conference of municipal treasurers in charge of managing a budget—no one thought of the money as their own.

Sadly, this experience is all too uncommon among Christians. In most Western nations, it's considered inappropriate to talk about your finances. In many circumstances, this is perfectly fitting. But there should also be a safe space where you can talk with other Christ-followers to discuss how best to steward money. That's what we've done with April and Craig Chapman (profiled in chapter 1): We gave them permission to see our annual record of expenses and to know everything about our net worth, our investment decisions, our finish line (our net worth target above which we would need no more savings), the amount we tithe—all of it. They did ask us to consider whether we were spending too much on our vacations, and we carefully considered their thoughts. In the end, we concluded we were spending the right amount, but we were grateful for their loving candor, and they readily accepted our answer.

We've also benefited tremendously from Generous Giving (https://generousgiving.org/), another fantastic organization dedicated to spreading the message of biblical generosity. They have a library of video profiles of generous givers on their website, including stories of a doctor who lives on a nurse's salary and gives away the difference and a business owner who handed over the ownership of his crane business to National Christian Foundation (he still runs the business and receives a salary, but the assets belong to the donor-advised fund and the profits fund Christian ministries). The stories aren't meant to be prescriptive, because God leads each of us differently; nor does Generous Giving guilt people into being generous. It's more like an invitation to live a joyful life.

That sense of infectious joy infuses gatherings of Christians committed to using all their resources for God's glory. Dour ascetics would feel deeply uncomfortable with the excitement and deep satisfaction that accompanies generosity. But this doesn't always come right away for everyone— it's a cultivated joy for some people. Dana will be quick to tell you that generosity is a learned virtue and one that she is growing into day by day. What began as an intellectual and moral commitment divorced from her emotions has become integrated and deeply joyful.

One of those people whose sense of purpose and joy flows freely from his being is Peter Greer.

Peter Greer: Combining Business, Poverty Alleviation, and Missions

Looking back, we see inflection points that changed the direction of our lives. For Bill, it was during a trip to Washington, DC, during his senior year in college, listening to then-Congressman Dan Coats (later a US Senator, ambassador to Germany, and director of National Intelligence) talk about being sold out for Christ even as he served in Congress. More than anything else, that speech shifted Bill's focus from overseas missions to a career in public policy in the White House and on Capitol Hill.

For Dana, it was when she was nineteen years old in a dirty, crowded, and noisy street in Madras, India, when an armless man covered in rags and sores leaned his head into her rickshaw with a beggar's cup in his mouth. Dana pulled away in fear and dread, and she immediately felt shame and conviction for her response. *How could I say I truly love the poor and needy, and then react in that manner?* Dana asked herself. She returned to the United States and promptly changed her college major to international development. Upon graduation, she looked up "international" in the Denver telephone book (something younger readers have never seen), which then launched her career in international trade policy for the US Department of Commerce and later international economic development for the US Agency for International Development and now for Impact Foundation.

For HOPE International president and CEO Peter Greer, the life-changing inflection point was a conversation in Moscow preceding his junior year at Messiah University. During an overseas program, Peter met a man who was working at the intersection of international business, poverty alleviation, and missions. "That was a defining moment of my life, and I can still picture the room. I immediately knew I wanted to be part of that type of work. I envisioned working for a Christ-centered economic development organization that was alleviating economic and spiritual poverty in challenging places around the world. That has become my life's work."

What a difference that conversation has made on the world! Almost thirty years later, HOPE International has 1,450 employees in twenty-five countries and has invested $1.6 billion in 2.7 million entrepreneurs' businesses. These entrepreneurs have leveraged small loans—as little as $20—to generate income to sustainably pay school fees, overcome food insecurity, access stable housing, and more—all in the name of Christ.

"I grew up seeing only doctors or church planters as potential missionaries. But I've since gained a much bigger understanding of missions that includes many other tools to advance the kingdom of God," Peter said.

It's not always made sense to everyone. "I remember meeting with one donor," Peter said. "As I got into the mechanics of how HOPE addresses poverty in the developing world, he said, 'This is too complicated. I'm out.' And he stood up and walked out of the room. What we do is outside the scope of traditional models of charity or aid."

HOPE's approach is different—and it's transformative. Ninety-seven percent of HOPE's loans are fully repaid with interest, though HOPE serves populations traditional banks won't reach.

By leaning heavily on a for-profit business model, HOPE International generates about $14 million in annual revenues from its many microloans to entrepreneurs in the developing world.

HOPE also raises money from donors to set up church-sponsored savings groups. "Savings groups provide vulnerable families with access to a safe place to save, small loans from their pooled savings, and a community to care for each other's needs. Where poverty has brought loneliness and isolation, savings groups foster Christ-centered community and support," heralds the HOPE website.

These savings groups become the full responsibility of the local church after three years, and 82 percent of them are still going after seven years.

"Our mission," said Peter, "involves Christ, community, and capital. And the capital part is where the American church has been absent in the past. But with important books like *When Helping Hurts* and *Toxic Charity*, the church is coming to see the role of development in advancing the kingdom of God." Peter has joined this movement to expand traditional understandings of "doing missions," coauthoring fifteen books that communicate his deep passion and vision for expanding Christ's kingdom.

Peter doesn't remember the name of the man working for the Mennonite Economic Development Associates in Russia—the one who first helped him see that business and missions fit together, which inspired him to go on to lead HOPE International after attaining a graduate degree from Harvard University. "I've tried to find him," Peter said. If that man is reading this book now, please know that through your timely word to a college junior thirty years ago, there are fewer people in extreme poverty and more Christ-followers today.

How Much to Give?

We believe the Bible is clear that tithing is still required in the New Testament. Jesus condemned the Pharisees for tithing all the way down to one-tenth of their spices yet neglecting justice, mercy, and faithfulness. He said, "You should have practiced the latter, without neglecting the former" (Matthew 23:23). That's good enough for us. Plus, we in the West are among the wealthiest people who have ever lived. If first-century farmers and shepherds could tithe, we certainly can!

The tithe isn't a ceiling, but a floor. We'd be hesitant to sanction giving more than 10 percent if you have outstanding debt for cars, education, or credit cards, but we would encourage you to consider setting out a plan for how you can meet your financial obligations and give more. Bill is very goal-oriented, and he's set a lifetime giving goal—it's ridiculously high, and he knows we may never get there, but just having a goal to strive for can keep you from thinking only of the next toy you can buy or the next milestone to hit in growing your net worth.

Our practice is to set annual giving percentage goals, increasing our tithe year over year as we've been able. As the kids have grown and moved out, we've been able to accelerate this growth. We've been inspired by the example of Robert LeTourneau, the wealthy twentieth-century inventor and manufacturer of earthmoving equipment, who did a reverse tithe of giving 90 percent and keeping only 10 percent for his own needs.

The Bible teaches us to bring the firstfruits (Nehemiah 10:37) of the harvest, which we interpret to mean we should tithe from our gross pay, not our net pay. In other words, God gets his cut before the taxman! Of course, the entire "cut" belongs to God, but the firstfruits devoted to the church universal come first.

Where to Give?

We have friends who are convinced that all charitable giving should go through the local church. However, we've never confined our giving just to the church and aren't persuaded this is a biblical requirement. We see the church universal as encompassing much more than just the local church. We are always careful to ensure we are giving an appropriate amount to our church so it's adequately funded, but we experience so much joy from giving to other ministries too. If you read the Bible differently, we respect your judgment.

If you give like we do, we recommend categorizing your giving so you can be intentional and planned, in keeping with the Lord's specific calling for your life. Our categories include the local church, evangelism, poverty, justice, cultural renewal, and stewardship, but you may have other categories. We've tended to balance where we give our money with where we contribute our time. For instance, Bill is heavily involved in the field of public justice and contributes many volunteer hours. As such, we give less money to those same causes. Giving takes many forms, so our categorization allows us to be thoughtful about where we give.

Leaving an Inheritance

Inheritance can be a blessing or a curse, and thinking through how much to leave behind and to whom requires great care. For many people, the default plan is to leave all their remaining wealth to the kids. We've been enormously blessed by an inheritance from Dana's father, and it launched our journey to explore stewardship more deeply. We've talked to many friends who are limiting how much they'll leave for their kids, preferring to pass on a legacy of generosity. Some people choose to help their kids "launch" by paying for all or part of college and graduate school and helping with a house down payment. That can help kids start their adult lives with minimal debt. Of course, for many families that's just not possible.

Obviously, there are no formulas for what you should bequeath and to whom, but these decisions should be bathed in prayer with the benefit of counsel from godly friends and then codified in your will.

David Wills: Creatively Finding New Ways to Steward Money

One of our own godly counselors has been David Wills, one of the preeminent pioneers of the modern generosity movement.

He scaled up a donor-advised fund called the National Christian Foundation from a fledgling organization that had granted less than $50 million in its first 15 years to one granting more than $21 billion twenty-five years later. He cofounded Generous Giving, a nonprofit that has catalyzed many millions of dollars in new charitable contributions. He also cofounded TrustBridge, a global network of donor-advised funds that has served 3,600 donors making more than five thousand grants valued at over $400 million to 1,100 organizations in more than one hundred countries. David has also served on the board of the Impact

Foundation from its outset, another donor-advised fund that has empowered donors to deploy half a billion dollars of their charitable capital to invest in for-profit businesses run according to Christian principles.

David is amazing.

But "Mr. Generosity" wasn't always so generous. "Generosity is not a natural inclination for me but a learned response," David said. "I always wanted to be wealthy. Although I won the parent lottery with two very generous parents, I grew up greedy."

David followed his propensity for argumentation and debate to law school and then into the courtroom. He loved litigation. He went from success to success and was enthusiastic about the future.

What moved David from a lucrative law practice into the nonprofit world? He met a man named Greg Sperry. "Greg shared his 'halftime' story of moving from being a litigator to serving Christian families in the trust, estate, and charitable areas," David told us. "He planted seeds that I, frankly, was hoping would not grow. He had lived in the litigation world, but something had changed, and his life looked completely different from mine in a way that eventually became irresistible. But like Jacob, I was wrestling with God. I fought Him for a year before I surrendered."

David's move from the partner track at a successful law firm into the nonprofit world is largely due to the fact that he "married up" with his wife, Chris. She has always cheered for David's move from a successful legal career to the far less lucrative field of nonprofit work. "My wife is an extravagantly generous person, and I wouldn't have made the move without her encouragement," David said.

Another turning point came when Greg asked David to read *Money, Possessions, and Eternity* by Randy Alcorn. "That book changed me," David said. "It was both heavy and exciting to read, but it's what shifted my perspective to an eternal mindset." David finally took the plunge, moving from his lucrative career to helping families flourish and ministries and churches thrive and grow.

"As we were helping very wealthy families direct billions of dollars into nonprofits, I knew there was no turning back. My hope is to lay up treasures in heaven and help others do the same. And I can honestly say I look back now without a single regret," David said. "God started to bless the work of our hands in just crazy ways."

As He did so, the Lord has led David to mentor scores of people who are similarly exploring changing their perspective from one of temporal riches to eternal riches. "Just as I was mentored, I am now blessed to encourage many other people—people who are going into very exciting places."

David told us,

The rapidly maturing generosity movement isn't recognizable today from where we were twenty-five years ago. Today it's global and breathtaking. More people today are thinking about setting a finish line [i.e., the point at which people cap their earnings and give the rest away] than ever before. They are not just asking, "How much can we give?" but are more and more often asking, "How much do we need to keep for our life-style?" The church is getting better at living out answers to three key questions: Why should I be generous, how should I do that, and where should I give? The flywheel is spinning faster and faster, and the gospel is spreading all over the world.

Has the path been easy? "Definitely not," David said. "We encountered many obstacles as we engaged in this spiritual battle. This was a huge threat to the Enemy." But the Lord has blessed David with close friends in the movement, people who made the otherwise difficult journey much more manageable.

David could have had a vastly different life than the one he has now. Instead of laying up treasure on earth, he desires to send it ahead to heaven. He took to heart Paul's words that "whoever sows sparingly will also reap sparingly, and whoever sows generously will also reap generously" (2 Corinthians 9:6). We suspect a bumper crop harvest awaits David in the life to come.

Stewarding wealth wisely requires intentionality. Among the practical steps to grow in stewarding money are:

1. Keep track of your expenses.
2. Live below your means.
3. Be cautious about taking on debt.
4. Get a wealth advisor schooled in biblical princi-ples who will help to align your investments with your faith.

5. Find friends with whom you can share openly about your financial decisions.

6. Tithe on your before-tax earnings and make plans to increase your giving, thoughtfully evaluating where you give.

7. Give special attention to how much you'll leave for your kids versus how much will be given away posthumously.

Fully Integrating Faith
and Finances

What is the chief end of man?
To glorify God and enjoy Him forever.
—Westminster Shorter Catechism, Q&A 1

The church is bursting at the seams with a fresh vigor for aligning our faith with how we use money—especially how we invest money. New organizations are springing up and thriving, many books are being written, podcasts are proliferating. The question is why it is happening now. Why not earlier?

The split between the sacred and the secular—the notion rooted in the ancient Gnostic vision that God cares only about spiritual things—has been tempting the church since its birth. Business has long been seen as something that happens outside the church, is less important than the real work of "full-time ministers," but is laudatory to the extent it funds evangelism and missions. This well-worn misunderstanding is beginning to fade as more people are awakening to the importance of using all our money in a way consistent with the biblical vision of *shalom*. *Shalom* is a Hebrew word usually translated as "peace," but its meaning extends beyond just the absence of conflict. *Shalom* also implies wholeness, completeness, prosperity, and well-being. God's economy is one of *shalom*, and it's our job to seek to establish it on earth.

But why now? Why didn't this happen earlier? We're not sure, nor is Mats Tunehag, who coined the phrase "business as mission" thirty years ago and has labored in the vineyards for a long time. "I don't know why it's happening now, but I'm thrilled to see it," Mats told us at a Faith Driven Entrepreneur meeting in the Washington, DC, metropolitan area recently.

There's still a long way to go before the movement to see the lordship of Christ reign over all financial dealings is fixed in the church's firmament. It will be necessary to convince pastors to stop using terms like *full-time Christian ministry* and similar terms that suggest that everyone else is in part-time ministry. The same is true of the word *worship* when it's used exclusively to mean time spent singing praise choruses and hymns and not also referring to the workweek—all of which should be worship to the extent it's done for God's glory. In the kingdom of God, there should be no part of our day that is not ministry. We're never off duty. Every breath we take should be under the Lord's command. Getting upstream to the seminaries will be important, exploding the compartmentalized theology elevating church work and diminishing all other work.

One of the first steps we took was hiring a financial advisor who was certified as a Kingdom Advisor,[36] thereby giving us tools and wisdom to integrate our finances with our faith. This need not be an all-or-nothing approach. Begin with a single step. In time, you'll find that you will think of your entire financial picture as a giant love letter to God. When you're making decisions about spending, saving, giving, and investing, you'll see it as just as much worship and ministry as your Bible reading and other church activities. You'll see that you're praising the Lord with all your life.

In time, you'll find that you will
think of your entire financial picture
as a giant love letter to God.

A Liturgy of Stewardship

We're not liturgical people, though we are members of an Anglican church that tests our low-church sensibilities. But Bill has developed his own liturgy that he says at the beginning of each day. It's designed to remind him he is a disciple and a steward, not an owner. It goes like this:

> You made me, You saved me, You own me, and You love me. There's nothing that I have that's not from

You; there's nothing I have that's not a gift. You are good, and I will choose to rejoice in the trials that come my way today because they give me the opportunity to become more like You. I will choose not to fear the future because You will be with me.

The prayer starts with "You made me," because that's fundamental to the Christian life. Before we were forgiven for our sins, we were made by Him and for Him. The fact that God created us means we owe Him our obedience. Some people think God is arrogant to demand our total allegiance—just who does He think He is? Well, He's God. If God didn't create us, then His demand for our servitude would be a power play—might makes right. But since He made us, we owe Him everything. In one way, our lives are a gift. Much more than that, however, our lives are a responsibility.

"You saved me." Saved from what? From our sin and the separation from God that it entails. God is totally other, totally good, and totally intolerant of rebellion—which is what sin is. The only way we can have a restored relationship with God is through Jesus's sacrifice on the cross and His resurrection from the dead. Our faith in the saving work of Christ demands our submission—not as a means of saving ourselves but as an expression of gratitude for God's grace.

"You own me." His creating us and then saving us means that He owns us. No other response would be appropriate. Full stop.

"You love me." This one is important. God is not a tyrant; He is the lover of our souls. Think of the person on earth who adores you the most, then infinitely multiply that love to understand God's affection for us. He wants what is best for us, and He wants us to flourish.

"There's nothing that I have that's not from You; there's nothing I have that's not a gift." What good gift do we have that we can't trace to God? Our parents, our genes, our daily food, our friends—they all come from God. He who created *ex nihilo* (out of nothing) is responsible for the goodness we enjoy. Recognizing our gifting leaves no room for arrogance or boasting and plants us in the fertile soil of gratitude. And gratitude is the secret ingredient to a life of joy.

"You are good, and I will choose to rejoice in the trials that come my way today because they give me the opportunity to become more like You." This one is challenging. We tend to measure our days by the extent to which things go the way we want them to go. But trials, disappointments, sickness, and other nasty things give us opportunities to be transformed into God's likeness. This sanctification happens only if we humbly submit to Him and His ways amid our suffering. And if it's true that we were made for God and to become like God, then our holiness is more important than living a life free of hardships. Suffering is not the *summum malum* (greatest evil); putting anything before God is.

"I will choose not to fear the future because You will be with me." We don't refuse to fear because we are guaranteed safety; we refuse to fear because God guarantees He will be with us until the "very end of the age" (Matthew 28:20). And if God is with us, then good can come from suffering (Genesis 50:20). Plus, what good is there in fearing what might happen? It's bad enough to experience adversity when it arrives, but there's no point in compounding our struggles by pre-living them. Shakespeare said, "Cowards die many times before their death; the valiant never taste of death but once."[37] And Jesus said, "Do not worry about tomorrow, for tomorrow will worry about itself. Each day has enough trouble of its own" (Matthew 6:34). Fear is often a misuse of our God-given imagination.

Henry Kaestner: Leading the Way in Aligning Faith and Capital

We end with one last story, this one from our friend and mentor Henry Kaestner. It would be difficult to overstate how much influence Henry has had driving forward the faith-driven investor and entrepreneur movement, building an organization that is unlocking millions of dollars to align with biblical values. Henry is a hero for us, a humble and farsighted man who loves God with all his heart and is passionate about seeing the Lord and His kingdom be exalted above all.

"I could afford a personal jet," Henry told us, "and I'd love to have one. But instead, I usually fly coach. For one thing, I know the Lord doesn't want me to have a jet. But I also know it would rob me of the joy I get from giving away money and investing in faith-driven businesses."

Henry Kaestner, a serial entrepreneur and venture capitalist, is a man with a mission. As the cofounder of

Bandwidth, now a publicly traded company with half a billion dollars in annual revenue and seven hundred employees, Henry knows how to succeed. In fact, success is all he's known in the business world.

Henry sees entrepreneurship flowing out of his innate love of solving problems. "I see a problem, and I work to provide a solution. And if the solution isn't big enough, I want to scale it until it is."

One of the big problems Henry sees is the need for Christians to align their private capital with their faith—and for entrepreneurs to integrate their faith into their businesses. To solve the problem, he cofounded Faith Driven Investor, "dedicated to helping Christ-following investors believe that God owns it all and that He cares deeply about the how, where, and why behind our investment strategies." He did the same with Faith Driven Entrepreneur, helping "entrepreneurs who are shaping culture to know God and look more like Him."

These sister organizations have trained more than twelve thousand entrepreneurs and investors from 122 countries in the principles of biblical stewardship. Their podcasts have been downloaded more than one million times. Henry Kaestner is helping deploy an army through his vision and devotion to inviting more Christ-followers to use all their talents to further the kingdom of God.

A striking thing about Henry is his passion for the Lord and his authenticity. Henry puts on no airs and he's humble. He's quick to concede what he doesn't know, and he's not afraid to admit his faults. He's intent on calling other

Christ-followers—a favorite term of Henry's that we now also use—to fully commit their financial resources to God. Henry's influence in our lives has been enormous. We listen to his podcasts and learn both about little-known investment concepts and real-life stories of Christians living out their faith in creative and exciting ways.

Henry began his public mission to integrate faith and capital by cofounding Sovereign's Capital in 2010. This asset manager has a family of funds in venture capital, private equity, and public equities. Henry's proving the thesis that investing should not be divorced from our faith in Christ—and it can be done without sacrificing market returns. "When 95 percent of the world's assets are in investments, not charitable giving, I look at investments as a way to solve problems," Henry said. "Charitable giving just won't fix the world's biggest problems."

Henry's parents were upper-middle-class, but they were frugal. "As a kid, I knew I wanted to be wealthy because my parents wouldn't let me buy Levi's jeans—they were too expensive. By age thirty, I had three and a half million dollars and thought it was all the money in the world. But quickly, God taught me that wealth isn't all I thought it was as a teenager," Henry said.

Henry and his wife, Kimberley, bought a beach house after one of Henry's early business successes. "But very soon thereafter I wanted more. I learned that wealth is never enough to make you happy," Henry said.

Early in their marriage, Henry and Kimberley had given their lives to the Lord. A few years later, Henry explained that he had a "born-again-again moment":

Even though we were giving away 20 percent of our income, the Lord showed me that He didn't need my money; He just wanted my heart. And once I understood that God owns it all, it took my faith life from black-and-white to technicolor. Once you realize that you don't own 80 percent, but you own nothing, you'd think that would be bad news. In fact, it frees you up to be a steward instead of an owner. It brings you joy in ways that you never expected.

This second conversion began a revolution in how Henry stewards his wealth. "While it's true that we give to be faithful and obedient, we also give out of joy and gratitude," he said.

Henry's latest joy is investing in entrepreneurs in Africa, where he's now helped to fund more than forty businesses. In addition to Africa being a promising market opportunity with a burgeoning population, Henry believes that what the continent needs more than handouts are businesses that provide jobs—jobs that alleviate and prevent poverty.

Henry is quick to acknowledge that he's financially very blessed and has never taken a vow of poverty. He is loath to call flying coach class *sacrificial*. "Perhaps the Lord will call me to sacrifice tomorrow, but we have been given so much. The key is to pray about our finances. Before we make any major purchase, we pray about it."

For Henry, financial stewardship is just another expression of living a sold-out life for Christ. "The way for me to get the desires of my heart is to draw closer to Him," he said.

Henry Kaestner is a man after God's own heart, and we are grateful for his leadership and example in our lives.

Joy in the Journey

It's easy to get caught on the hamster wheel of pleasure and money and things. Many people learn too late that their appetites are insatiable and that they won't find the lasting joy that comes from using resources to love God and neighbor. We hope this book has been for you an invitation to joy, not drudgery, because that's exactly what we heard from the many people we interviewed.

Many people learn too late that their appetites are insatiable and that they won't find the lasting joy that comes from using resources to love God and neighbor.

The interviews turned out to be the best part about writing the book. We heard amazing stories of faithful stewardship, and we felt a keen sense of responsibility to capture in words these beautiful lives lived unto God. Since it's impossible to capture everything in just eight hundred words, the metanarrative of the twenty-four stories consisted of eight dominant themes:

1. Humility. These weren't people crowing about their accomplishments. To the contrary, we had to coax out of them their stories of achievement and sacrifice, reminding them that readers want to hear about how God has worked in their lives.

2. Focus on others. Each person had a deep sense of others' needs. Tim Keller wrote that "the essence of gospel-humility is not thinking more of myself or thinking less of myself, it is thinking of myself less."[38]

3. Light and easy yokes. Although each person had made substantial sacrifices to pursue their calling, there wasn't a sense of heaviness or deprivation. Instead, each person seemed amazed at how much they have even after giving to others. When we praised them for their faithful obedience, they wanted to correct us, explaining how much the Lord has given them and how light their sacrifices have been.

4. Gratitude. Everyone was filled with gratitude for God's blessings in their lives.

5. Joy. These people are joyful givers. They feel they are privileged to be able to participate in God's work.

6. Agency. People recognize they're part of God's grand design in the world, actors on the cosmic stage seeking to further the kingdom of God through their lives. They see themselves as world-changers, not in a grandiose way, because they know their works have a small impact relative to the needs, but they see that their lives make a difference in others' lives.

7. No dour ascetics. There was no sense of guilt-induced activity to make themselves worthy of salvation; rather, they demonstrated a sense of joyful and grateful response to the gifts they had been given.

8. "Well done." People repeatedly quoted Jesus's parable in which the person heard the words "Well done, good and faithful servant," reflecting the palpable yearning among the interviewees (Matthew 25:21).

Everyone is a sinner, but there is an incessant focus on Christians' shortcomings and too little celebration of those faithfully living obedient lives of joyful service. The stories in this book weren't sugarcoated for effect. If anything, space prevented us from sharing even more of the good things we heard.

There is joy in surrendering all that you are, including your finances, to the lordship of Christ. Taking those first steps can feel a bit scary and even onerous, but that's not where it ends. In laying down our lives and the endless pursuit of wealth and comfort, Christ-followers can embrace the joyful and invigorating life of service and purpose, tangibly experiencing that it is better to give than to receive.

We pray that your dreams will be transformed into how you can free the captive, equip the entrepreneur, and open wide the gates of life experienced to the full—precisely what our friends whose stories we captured in this book are doing.

With each breath you take, you have the potential to write a love letter to God.

Write it well.

APPENDIX A

Getting Started on Your Stewardship Journey

I f you're ready to go deeper in your stewardship journey, here are some practical steps to pursue:

1. Study the Bible's teachings on finances (see www .crown.org to get started).

2. Regularly pray about your finances. God cares about all of it.

3. Read a book, listen to a podcast, and join an online discussion group about financial stewardship. Appendix B has a wealth of recommended resources.

4. Keep a record of all your spending, savings, giving, and investing for one year. Buy a software program to make it easier. We use Quicken.

5. Create a budget based on your actual spending with realistic and necessary adjustments to live below your means. Use a budgeting app such as YNAB or EveryDollar, and rely on resources from Crown Ministries, Ron Blue, Howard Dayton, or others. You'll find these in appendix B.

6. Research your relative wealth by global standards. Acknowledge what you've been given.

7. Tithe at least 10 percent of your before-tax income.

8. Strive to save at least 10 percent annually.

9. Pay off your consumer debt and aim to be debt-free.

10. Set long-term saving, investing, and giving goals.

11. Share your financial details with a wise and godly trusted confidante.

12. Hire a Kingdom Advisor (https://kingdomadvisors .com/) who can help you begin the process of aligning your investable assets with your faith.

13. Open a donor-advised fund at National Christian Foundation or another trusted institution.

14. Observe the Sabbath each week.

15. Draw up your will with an attorney or an online service. Be sure it's legally sound.

16. Set a finish line for your net worth and your annual spending/saving.

17. Be prepared to make mistakes. Don't give up. The Lord is pleased that you're seeking to bring all your resources to His feet to be used for His purposes.

APPENDIX B

Resources

What's the definition of an intellectual? Someone who's forgotten who their sources are! In the same way, there's nothing we know that we haven't learned from others—even if we think the idea is ours. The below organizations, podcasts, blogs, books, and videos have shaped our thoughts around stewardship. There are undoubtedly many other excellent resources beyond these.

Organizations, Podcasts, Videos, and Blogs

Founded by Henry Kaestner (profiled in chapter 9), the Faith Driven Investor (www.faithdriveninvestor.org) features a podcast, videos, and a blog with amazing stories from investors who are aligning their capital with their faith. You can also join a small group (virtually or in person) for a six-week study with fellow investors. We are deeply indebted to FDI.

The Faith Driven Entrepreneur website (https://www.faith drivenentrepreneur.org) has a podcast, videos, and a blog, employing the power of story to speak into the heart of the opportunities and challenges in front of all entrepreneurs. You can also join a small group (virtually or in person) for an eight-week study with fellow entrepreneurs. This organization was also founded by Henry Kaestner.

Generous Giving (https://generousgiving.org), led by our friend April Chapman (profiled in chapter 1), spreads the message of biblical generosity, especially among those entrusted with much. Founded in 2000 by the Maclellan Foundation, it was launched with a vision to stir a renewed, Spirit-led commitment to generosity among followers of Christ through conversation.

National Christian Foundation (NCF, www.ncfgiving .com) is a donor-advised fund (DAF) helping givers mobilize resources by inspiring biblical generosity. They have a huge library of resources. We love how NCF has helped us give more by using creative tax strategies. We faithfully read their Saturday email digest and rely on their expertise in growing into greater generosity.

Praxis (https://www.praxislabs.org/) is a venture-building ecosystem with a redemptive imagination, supporting founders, funders, and innovators motivated by their faith to address the major issues of our time. They have a journal and podcast, and they offer courses on "redemptive entrepreneurship." Praxis was influential in starting us on the journey connecting our faith and our capital.

The Gathering (www.thegathering.com) is an annual meeting of Christian philanthropists seeking to build community with others in a common desire to follow the Lord in every aspect of their lives, from giving to earning to investing to hospitality—everything. We have been deeply blessed hearing Gathering members' stories, some of which appear in the pages of this book.

The Lion's Den DFW (http://www.thelionsdendfw.org/) and The Lion's Den Birmingham (https://www.thelionsden.us/) were created to fuel the expansion of the kingdom economy through investing in transformative entrepreneurship. Through their annual conferences and pitch competitions, they connect and equip business leaders to use their wealth and experience to change the world and create a tremendous impact. Their goal is to facilitate values-aligned investments by connecting Christ-centered entrepreneurs with investors.

Christian Economic Forum (https://christianeconomicforum.com/) is a global platform and international community for leaders to collaborate and introduce strategic ideas for spreading God's economic principles and the goodness of Jesus Christ. We attend their annual conference and have built many rich relationships with like-minded Christ-followers.

Women Doing Well (https://womendoingwell.org/) helps high-net-worth women explore and discover their divine purpose and path into lifestyle generosity.

Crown Financial Ministries (https://www.crown.org/) helps people become responsible financial stewards using biblical methods and resources to transform individuals, families, communities, and even entire nations. We have been Crown devotees since we were engaged to be married and have continued to rely on their resources to steward the financial resources we've been given. Their website is filled with useful and accessible resources to help you get started on your stewardship journey.

Compass (https://compass1.org/) is a ministry dedicated to teaching people God's way of handling their resources, working in about seventy countries worldwide. The Finish Line podcast (https://www.finishlinepledge.com/podcast/), cohosted by Kealan Hobelmann (a surgeon) and his brother Cody Hobelmann (a financial advisor), addresses the intersection of faith, generosity, and personal finance with a variety of guests, including pastors, financial advisors, radically generous givers, entrepreneurs, CEOs, and nonprofit leaders to explore the question of how best to steward God's wealth.

The Ascendants podcast (Spotify, Apple) with Kate Gardner (profiled in chapter 3) features descendants of financially successful families who are ascending into their own identities and impact. Guests share how they came to terms with and eventually took stewardship of their family legacy.

Investing with Integrity podcast (https://investing-with
-integrity.captivate.fm/) covers Biblically Responsible
Investing (BRI), empowering people to align financial and
moral goals.

The Generous Business Owner podcast (https://www
.generousbusinessowner.com/) features business owners
Jeff Thomas, Alan Barnhart, and Jeff Rutt (profiled in
chapter 5) and their guests discussing practical ways to be
more generous.

The Faith & Work podcast (https://www.denverinstitute
.org/podcasts/) explores everyday work in God's world.
Through conversations with organizational leaders, front-
line workers, and scholars across industries, it tackles common workplace challenges, broadens your vision for how
God is at work in our communities, and offers tools to
deepen your experience of God on the job.

The Faith & Co. documentary film series and courses
from Seattle Pacific University (https://faithandco.spu.edu)
highlight the struggles and triumphs of people living out
business as their calling. Filmed across three continents in a
wide range of industries, these inspiring examples provoke
questions and provide insights about how to act as a faithful follower of Christ in business.

Eventide Center for Faith and Investing (https://www
.faithandinvesting.com/podcast) offers courses, podcasts,
and a journal about why and how to integrate investing
with Christian faith.

The Kingdom Investor podcast (https://thekingdominvestor
.buzzsprout.com/) features personal stories from business
leaders who have moved from success to significance, sharing how they use worldly wealth for kingdom impact.

Christian Wealth Management (https://www.investforthe
gloryofgod.com/podcast) has a podcast that explores the
intersection of faith and finance.

Christians for Impact (www.christiansforimpact.org)
includes a podcast and blog to help analytically minded
Christians pursue vocations with real and radical impact
on pressing global problems.

Business as Mission (www.businessasmission.com) makes
plain God's redemptive work through business in the world.
BAM has a blog, a podcast, and a wealth of publications.

The Feast over Famine Podcast (https://www.feastover
famine.org/podcast) features stories about social enterprise
and business for transformation projects globally. The conversations are with founders, CEOs, impact investors, and
other stakeholders in the social enterprise ecosystem.

The Generosity Now Podcast (https://www.generositynow
.org/) is dedicated to inspiring generosity and promoting
whole-life stewardship among followers of Christ, sharing
stories of individuals and organizations doing great work in
their communities and around the world.

Sovereign's Capital (https://sovereignscapital.com) provides capital and strategic partnership to companies and

funds led by faith-driven teams that have the potential for outsize returns and impact. They invest directly in profitable, lower-middle-market companies, in early stage technology companies across seed and Series A stages, in publicly traded companies, and in domestic real estate with a primary focus on value-add strategies. They also use a fund of funds strategy to invest in venture and private equity fund managers through primaries, secondaries, co-investments, and GP stakes. Most important, Sovereign's exists to love God and neighbor through investing. Founded by Henry Kaestner.

Talanton (https://www.talantonllc.com) invests in values-driven, growth-stage businesses in low-income countries to create jobs, bring hope, and combat poverty. You can invest directly or from your donor-advised fund. Founder David Simms (featured in chapter 5) leads Talanton, and Dana serves on their board.

Kingdom Advisors (https://kingdomadvisors.com/) equips financial advisors to help their clients begin the process of aligning their investable assets with their faith.

The SENT Network (https://www.sentventures.com/) helps Catholic business leaders integrate their faith with their work.

Generous Family (https://generousfamily.com) seeks to empower families to teach children the habit of generosity. Their site has a host of resources, including books, videos, and a homeschool curriculum.

We also encourage you to check out the Bible Project's video "Generosity" (https://bibleproject.com/explore/video /generosity/).

Books

Anne R. Bradley and Art Lindsley, eds. *For the Least of These: A Biblical Answer to Poverty* (Zondervan, 2014). This biblically grounded book provides a defense of caring for the poor through sustainable economic development rooted in markets and trade.

Chuck Bentley, *The Root of Riches: What If Everything You Think About Money Is Wrong?* (Blackstone Publishing, 2020). Bentley encourages an honest look into the core values of our lives and our view of wealth. We love Chuck's leadership in Christian Economic Forum and Crown Financial Ministries.

David Green with Bill High, *Giving It All Away . . . and Getting It All Back Again: The Way of Living Generously* (Zondervan, 2017). Founder of America's craft store giant Hobby Lobby, Green unpacks biblical principles that help others reap the benefits of generosity and build a lasting legacy.

David Wills, Terry Parker, and Greg Sperry, *Family. Money: Five Questions Every Family Should Ask About Wealth* (National Christian Foundation, 2018). These founding pioneers in the generosity movement will help you think through a family stewardship philosophy.

Donald E. Simmons, *The Steward Investor: Investing God's Resources for Eternal Impact* (Innovo Publishing, 2022). Our friend Don Simmons (featured in chapter 7) makes a compelling case for Christ-followers to invest holistically according to kingdom principles.

Henry Kaestner, ed., *Faith Driven Investing: Every Investment Has an Impact—What's Yours?* (Tyndale Momentum, 2023). Our mentor and role model Henry Kaestner (profiled in chapter 9) coauthors and edits this book that makes the case for aligning our investing with our faith in Christ, envisioning how our capital can grow and fund God's purposes in the world.

Howard Dayton, *Building Your Finances God's Way* (Compass, 2021). Dayton is the founder of Crown Ministries and a pioneer in integrating faith and finances.

John Cortines and Gregory Baumer, *God and Money: How We Discovered True Riches at Harvard Business School* (Rose Publishing, 2016). A compelling story of how the two authors experienced the rewards of radical generosity, providing theological lessons and practical examples. Greg's story is in chapter 3.

John Cortines and Gregory Baumer, *True Riches: What Jesus Really Said About Money and Your Heart* (Thomas Nelson, 2019).

John Rinehart, *Gospel Patrons: People Whose Generosity Changed the World* (Reclaimed Publishing, 2016). We love this book about mostly forgotten people who financially equipped well-known leaders in their calling.

Ken Blanchard and S. Truett Cathy, *The Generosity Factor: Discover the Joy of Giving Your Time, Talent, and Treasure* (Zondervan, 2002). In the tradition of the best-selling book *The One Minute Manager*, Blanchard and Cathy (entrepreneur and founder of Chick-fil-A) tell a parable of a business owner who demonstrates the virtues of generosity.

Curt Laird, *The Culture Key: Successful Investing and Entrepreneurship in Frontier and Emerging Markets* (Xana Publishing, 2018). Curt (profiled in chapter 7) explores the idea that entrepreneurs and investors in frontier and emerging markets struggle not because they lack business acumen but because they do not develop intercultural intelligence.

Leo Tolstoy, *How Much Land Does a Man Need?* (The Trinity Forum, 2011). Written in 1886, this short story powerfully tells the story of a man who forfeits everything in his desire to acquire land.

Peter Greer and Phil Smith, *Created to Flourish: How Employment-Based Solutions Help Eradicate Poverty* (Hope International, 2017). Greer and Smith draw on their personal experiences to discuss proven solutions for effectively alleviating poverty.

Praxis Labs, *Redemptive Investing: A Playbook for Leaders* (Praxis, 2023). This is an awesome little book from our friends at Praxis.

Praxis Labs, *The Redemptive Business: A Playbook for Leaders* (Praxis, 2021). This is another great primer from Praxis, which has mentored us in our own stewardship journey.

Randy Alcorn, *Money, Possessions, and Eternity: A Comprehensive Guide to What the Bible Says About Financial Stewardship, Generosity, Materialism, Retirement, Financial Planning, Gambling, Debt, and More* (Tyndale House, 2021). Alcorn's practical and comprehensive biblical study about money and possessions.

Randy Alcorn, *The Law of Rewards: Giving What You Can't Keep to Gain What You Can't Lose* (Tyndale Momentum, 2003). Alcorn makes a compelling case for a biblical perspective on stewardship. We love Alcorn and his godly wisdom.

Randy Alcorn, *The Treasure Principle: Unlocking the Secret of Joyful Giving*, revised and updated edition (Multnomah, 2017). Alcorn demonstrates through myriad biblical texts the key role generosity plays in the Christian life, both to the believer's joy and for the fruit it generates on earth and for eternity.

Raymond Harris, *Enduring Wealth: Being Rich in This World and the Next* (BroadStreet Publishing Group, 2024). Harris shares how he has seen God multiply human efforts when people faithfully steward all God has given them.

Ron Blue with Jeremy White, *Splitting Heirs: Giving Your Money and Things to Your Children Without Ruining Their Lives* (Northfield Publishing, 2008). Blue and White argue that the financial wealth you leave behind could be the best thing that ever happened to your loved ones—or the worst.

Ronald Sider, *Rich Christians in an Age of Hunger: Moving from Affluence to Generosity* (Thomas Nelson, 2015). This book was hugely consequential for us when we were young adults.

Steven Garber, *Visions of Vocation: Common Grace for the Common Good* (InterVarsity Press Books, 2014). Steve Garber has been very influential in our thinking over three decades, and this book captures the biblical vision for full integration of faith and life.

Todd Harper, *Abundant: Experiencing the Incredible Journey of Generosity* (Generous Giving, 2016). *Abundant* helps you consider the role of money in your personal journey and in the kingdom of God.

Timothy Keller, *Counterfeit Gods: The Empty Promises of Money, Sex, and Power, and the Only Hope That Matters* (Viking, 2009). Keller shows how a proper understanding of the Bible reveals the unvarnished truth about societal ideals and our own hearts. We're huge Keller fans.

APPENDIX C

Summing Up

We love making lists. The lists below encapsulate what we've tried to communicate in the book. First, here are the foundational ideas we believe:

1. God owns everything. Everything we have is God's, even if we hold the deed. That's not to say we haven't worked hard to earn what we have, but even the ability to work hard we trace back to God, because "every good and perfect gift is from above" (James 1:17).

2. We are accountable to God. One day, we will stand before God to give account for how we used our money and other resources He put on loan to us, and we want Him to be pleased. We don't want to hear the words, "I gave you so much, but you were self-indulgent." God's kingdom is eternal, and

ours is temporary—but our choices have eternal implications. We yearn to have an abundance . . . in heaven!

3. God's kingdom is all-encompassing. There is nothing about which God is indifferent. Many people put a heavy focus on the Great Commission, but they pay little attention to the Creation Mandate and the Cultural Commission. We are meant to flourish in all aspects, bearing fruit and multiplying. The kingdom of God is about more than just saving souls. It's about mending that which is broken and striving for the *shalom* we knew in Eden—including in business and financial stewardship.

4. You must dethrone money. Jesus said, "Where your treasure is, there your heart will be also," and a few verses later, "You cannot serve both God and money" (Matthew 6:21, 24). Author Andy Crouch explains that serving money is truly serving a demonic power that wants to have mastery over us in lieu of God.[39] It's an either-or situation. Living generously is the best way we have discovered to dethrone money in our lives.

Those are the big ideas that shape our views. Their general applications include the following:

1. Be generous. God is generous with us, and we should be generous to emulate Him. Remember Jesus's parable about the servant whose heavy debts were forgiven by his master but who then mercilessly demanded a fellow servant repay a small debt

(Matthew 18:21–35)? Christ-followers have been forgiven much, and we dare not be stingy.

2. Align your money with your faith. God cares about everything, including the ends and the means, and He cares about businesses in which we invest (and that's what we're doing with our money when we put it in the stock market). We know He doesn't want us to be drug dealers just so we can tithe on the income, and He doesn't want us to invest in businesses that corrupt the world.

3. Money lies. It can lead us to think we're in control of our lives when He wants to be in control. He wants us to put our hope and our confidence in Him, not in our bank account or our net worth.

4. Money is a dangerous blessing. Loving money more than God is wrong, but enjoying and being grateful for the money the Lord has given us is good. We need to fix in our minds that God comes before money and live accordingly.

5. Poverty isn't inherently good. Some people are called to live in poverty, and their obedience is pleasing to the Lord, but it's not necessarily better than wealth. The question is being faithful with what we have, whether it's a lot or a little.

6. Work pleases God. All work done according to God's will and in His name is holy and sanctifying. We were made to work. Work preceded the fall, and we'll work in heaven. Leisure should be hemmed in. We should rest in order to work, not work in order to rest. There's a reason God commanded us

to work six days and rest one day—it redounds to our benefit.

7. Stewardship pleases God. It's not necessarily a way to get rich. We might be righteously poor or unjustly rich. Want and suffering come to everyone, though not equally. The health-and-wealth gospel is an oxymoron.

8. God loves risk-taking. Risk helps us flourish. The success or failure of an enterprise is in God's keeping. Our duty is to faithfully follow His call, including in taking risks.

9. Pray about money. We should steward our money by seeking God's guidance in prayer. What He's commanded our neighbor to do isn't necessarily our call. We need to talk to and listen to God to discern His will for us. One person can drive a Mercedes in great joy and in keeping with God's call, and another person can't even own a car in obedience to God.

10. Don't walk alone. We should steward our money with accountability. We shouldn't make such important decisions in a vacuum. It's not helpful that people are so private about their money. We have found some godly friends with whom we can talk specifics about our financial stewardship. Greed, like mushrooms, grows best in the dark. We try to bring light to our money management.

11. Save, but don't hoard. The Bible is critical both of people who hoard wealth and of people who fail

to save for the future. Finding the balance can be tricky, but it can be done.

12. God loves both multiplication and addition. The Good Shepherd leaves the ninety-nine sheep to look for the lost one (addition), but God also calls us to flourish and multiply—and that means much more than having babies! Profit is built into creation as we see crops grow after planting or livestock multiplying, though the fall has too often twisted it into exploitation. God loves for-profit businesses—and not just to support missionaries. Business can be a powerful agent of God's kingdom, mending, healing, and bringing hope and joy to people whom it serves.

13. The sacred/secular split has infected our view of money. To God, nothing is secular—all can be made holy and good (aside from specific activities that He forbids). "Calling" isn't limited to pastors and missionaries but includes businesspeople and ballplayers, artists, architects—and everyone else.

14. God loves giving and investing. Both can be beautiful to God and can serve His purposes when they're done for His glory. Investing is not just a way to earn money so we can give.

Now for some specific applications of what we believe:

1. You're probably rich. Most people in the West are rich by global standards, though many people don't see themselves that way. It's important to recognize

our comparative wealth to understand our responsibility. Jesus said, "From everyone who has been given much, much will be demanded" (Luke 12:48), but it's hard to realize what's been demanded of us if we don't first recognize how much we've been given.

2. Money can corrupt. It can lead us to be greedy, lazy, addicted to luxuries, arrogant, and exploitive. Money is dangerous, and regular self-examination of our use of money is critical to becoming good stewards.

3. The tithe should be a floor, not a ceiling. The tithe should be our firstfruits—meaning it should be done before we pay our taxes.

4. Live below your means. Save money. There's a difference between trusting God and failing to prepare for the unexpected. Many people in the West are expecting nothing bad to happen to them and live paycheck to paycheck, which is irresponsible and makes them end up depending on their family or the government to support them. This isn't godly; it's wrong.

5. Donor-advised funds (DAFs) are awesome. You may not have heard of them before reading this book, but DAFs are powerful tools to creatively deploy your charitable capital for both grants to nonprofits and investments in for-profit businesses that hopefully will return the capital with interest so it can be granted or reinvested elsewhere. DAFs enable us to increase the impact of our charitable dollars. (We explain in chapter 5.)

6. Don't stop working. Once we've earned enough that we don't need to work for pay anymore, then we will continue working and giving away everything we earn. Retirement shouldn't become full-time leisure.

7. Don't be a workaholic. We should observe the Sabbath by making a day of rest integral to our weekly routines. Our principal identity should not come from our jobs but from Christ.

8. Pray through financial decisions. The question shouldn't only be whether we *could* afford something but whether we *should* afford something. We commit to doing whatever the Lord leads us to do, even if it's hard.

9. Record your spending, giving, saving, and investing. We strive to be intentional about our stewardship. It's easy to deceive ourselves, and regular recordkeeping sheds light on what we do, not just what we intend to do.

10. Bequeath generosity. We're careful about leaving too much money for our children. It's better to leave a legacy of generosity than a huge inheritance.

11. Set giving goals. We try to subvert our acquisitive tendencies by channeling them into generosity. We dream about more than sailboats and vacations; we dream about ways to lift people out of poverty.

12. Avoid consumer debt. We're cautious about debt, especially consumer debt. We made it our goal to be debt-free (which we are). There is enormous freedom in owing nothing.

ACKNOWLEDGMENTS

This book, like all books, reflects the accumulated wisdom of many people who have graciously invested in our lives. We love learning from others, and our book was born out of countless conversations, books, small groups, webinars, and seeing firsthand how ordinary people are living out extraordinary lives.

When politicians address a crowded room of supporters, they're often loath to begin singling out people for praise lest they forget someone. We run the same risk, but fools rush in where angels fear to tread. Here goes . . .

We're indebted to Dennis and Eileen Bakke for setting us on the path of financial stewardship through their adult Sunday school lessons almost forty years ago. Their transparent modeling of what it means to be stewards inspires us.

April and Craig Chapman have been models and guides in stewarding our increasing resources for the past ten years. We're so glad we "coincidentally" met them at The Gathering, and they opened their lives to us.

Henry Kaestner has been our rock star, and we're the heads of his fan club. Henry winsomely and passionately lives a life surrendered to Jesus, personally contributing a significant portion of his wealth to spreading the message of faith-driven investing.

Brian Fikkert's book *When Helping Hurts* has been instrumental in reshaping our thoughts about the best way to empower the poor.

The late Larry Burkett's books were so important to us. Larry went home in 2003. His teachings helped us unify our approach to finances as a young couple, avoiding many of the otherwise common fights around money.

As young adults, we were heavily impacted by the late Ron Sider's book *Rich Christians in an Age of Hunger*, which sensitized us to world poverty relative to Western wealth.

David Simms at Talanton is a trailblazer in directing investments to small- and medium-sized businesses in East Africa, creating jobs with dignity in the name of Christ.

Chuck Bentley's founding and leadership of Christian Economic Forum has brought us into a community of like-minded Christ-followers seeking to solve difficult economic problems worldwide.

We're grateful to Gisle Sorli, our Kingdom Advisor at Keel Point, for helping us align our public stock holdings with our faith and for helping us think through a responsible point at which to reach our "finish line"—when we could begin giving away all our earnings.

We're indebted to the early readers of our manuscript, including Joel Steindel, Rob Schwarzwalder, John Coleman,

Michael Lehmann, Josh Kwan, and David Simms. Forefront's editor, Allen Harris, helped us improve the wording and the flow of the book.

And like the Tomb of the Unknown Soldier, special thanks to those people whom we'll remember after the book is already in print!

NOTES

1. Ronald J. Sider, *Rich Christians in an Age of Hunger* (Word Publishing, 1990).
2. *Forbes* magazine's "Richest People in America List" in 2000.
3. "The Disinheritors," *Forbes*, May 19, 1997, https://www.forbes.com/forbes/1997/0519/5910152a.html.
4. The Great Commission is Jesus's final admonition before returning to heaven, calling us to make disciples. This is important, but it's not our only task.
5. Charles Colson and Nancy Pearcey, *How Now Shall We Live?* (Wheaton, IL: Tyndale House, 1999), XII.
6. Andy Crouch, "As for Me and My Household, We'll Resist Mammon," *Christianity Today*, April 18, 2022, https://www.christianitytoday.com/ct/2022/may-june/crouch-money-home-me-my-household-resist-mammon-community.html.
7. The IRS website describes a donor-advised fund (DAF) as "a separately identified fund or account that is maintained and operated by a section 501(c)(3) organization, which is called a sponsoring organization. Each account is composed of contributions made by individual donors. Once

the donor makes the contribution, the organization has legal control over it. However, the donor, or the donor's representative, retains advisory privileges with respect to the distribution of funds and the investment of assets in the account." See "SOI Tax Stats: Definitions of Selected Terms and Concepts for Tax-Exempt Organizations," IRS, accessed September 28, 2024, https://www.irs.gov/statistics /soi-tax-stats-definitions-of-selected-terms-and-concepts -for-tax-exempt-organizations#:~:text=Donor%2DAdvised %20Funds—Generally%2C,contributions%20made %20by%20individual%20donors.

8. A DAF is a nonprofit entity that receives charitable donations that are put into an account under the name of the donor. The donor is then permitted to advise the DAF on how the funds in their account will be donated or invested. The money you put in a DAF is no longer yours to own, but you can decide where it's given or how it's invested.

9. This is not necessarily prescriptive; it is simply descriptive of the Chapmans' journey.

10. Sonja Lyubomirsky, Kennon M. Sheldon, and David Schkade, "Pursuing Happiness: The Architecture of Sustainable Change," *Review of General Psychology* 9, no. 2 (2005): 111–31.

11. Frederick Buechner, *Wishful Thinking: A Theological ABC* (Harper & Row, 1973), 95.

12. Charles Colson and Nancy Pearcey, *How Now Shall We Live?* (Wheaton, IL: Tyndale House, 1999), XII.

13. Reproduced with small edits from our posting, "How Budgeting Increases the Joy of Giving," National Christian

Foundation, January 17, 2019, https://www.ncfgiving.com /stories/how-budgeting-increases-the-joy-of-giving/.

14. Will Kenton, "Profit Definition Plus Gross, Operating, and Net Profit Explained," Investopedia, updated June 12, 2024, https://www.investopedia.com/terms/p/profit.asp#:~:text =Profit%20describes%20the%20financial%20benefit ,sustaining%20the%20activity%20in%20question.

15. Jim Collins and Jerry I. Porras, *Built to Last: Successful Habits of Visionary Companies* (New York: HarperBusiness, 1994), 55.

16. Ronald Reagan, "Remarks on East-West Relations at the Brandenburg Gate in West Berlin," June 12, 1987, The American Presidency Project, https://www.reagan foundation.org/media/128814/brandenburg.pdf.

17. James D. Bratt, ed., *Abraham Kuyper: A Centennial Reader* (Eerdmans, 1998), 488.

18. The Lilly Foundation, Giving 2024 (Lilly Foundation, 2024).

19. "The USA Wealth Report 2024," Henley & Partners, accessed August 8, 2024, https://www.henleyglobal.com /publications/usa-wealth-report-2024.

20. George Eliot, *Middlemarch* (Penguin Classics, 1994), 578.

21. Os Guinness, *The Call: Finding and Fulfilling the Central Purpose of Your Life* (W Publishing, 1998), 71.

22. "Is Charitable Giving Resilient? Or Stagnant?," Giving USA, July 5, 2023, https://givingusa.org/is-charitable-giving -resilient-or-stagnant/#:~:text=The%20most%20troubling %20is%20a,a%20charitable%20gift%20each%20year.

23. Irenaeus, *Adversus Haereses* 4.20.7.

24. This is not an ironclad rule of life. Good businesses run according to kingdom principles can still fail. There is no one-to-one correlation between virtue and success.

25. "What Is Redemptive Entrepreneurship?" Praxis, accessed April 26, 2024, https://www.praxislabs.org/redemptive -entrepreneurship.

26. Madalyn Hayden, "Recidivism Rates in the United States Versus Europe: How and Why Are They Different?" (honors thesis, Western Michigan University, 2023), 1, https:// scholarworks.wmich.edu/cgi/viewcontent.cgi?article =4677&context=honors_theses#:~:text=The%20United %20States%20has%20a,at%2020%25%20within%205 %20years.

27. Randy Alcorn, "Will We Work and Have Jobs in Heaven?," Eternal Perspective Ministries, September 7, 2018, https:// www.epm.org/resources/2018/Sep/7/will-we-work-and -have-jobs-heaven/.

28. Chenkai Wu, Michelle C. Odden, Gwenith G. Fisher, and Robert S. Stawski, "Association of Retirement Age with Mortality: A Population-Based Longitudinal Study Among Older Adults in the USA," *Journal of Epidemiology and Community Health* 70, no. 9 (March 21, 2016): 917–23. https://doi.org/10.1136/jech-2015-207097.

29. Jack Flynn, "Average Global Income [2023]: What Is the Median Income Worldwide?," Zippia, April 13, 2023, https:// www.zippia.com/advice/average-income-worldwide/.

30. Gloria Guzman and Melissa Kollar, "Income in the United States: 2022," United States Census Bureau, September 12, 2023, https://www.census.gov/library/publications /2023/demo/p60-279.html#:~:text=Real%20median %20household%20income%20was,and%20Table%20A %2D1).

31. Guzman and Kollar, "Income."

32. John Coleman and Luke Roush, hosts, Faith Driven Investor, episode 137, "The Steward Investor with Don Simmons," Faith Driven Investor, December 12, 2022, https://www.faithdriveninvestor.org/podcast-inventory/episode-137-the-steward-investor-with-don-simmons.

33. "How Rich Am I?," Giving What We Can, accessed September 28, 2024, https://www.givingwhatwecan.org/how-rich-am-i.

34. Andy Crouch, *Strong and Weak: Embracing a Life of Love, Risk, and True Flourishing* (InterVarsity Press, 2016), 147.

35. "Quarterly Report on Household Debt and Credit," Center for Microeconomic Data, Federal Reserve Bank of New York, released August 2023, https://www.newyorkfed.org/medialibrary/interactives/householdcredit/data/pdf/HHDC_2023Q2.

36. Financial advisors aren't just for the wealthy. They're affordable for all since they harvest approximately one percent of your earnings, so you never have to dole out cash to pay them. In our experience, they more than pay for themselves.

37. William Shakespeare, *Julius Caesar*, act 2, scene 2, line 32.

38. Timothy Keller, *The Freedom of Self-Forgetfulness: The Path to True Christian Joy* (10Publishing, 2012), 32.

39. Crouch, "As for Me."

INDEX